Solved by Sunset

Solved
by
Sunset

*The Right-Brain Way
to Resolve Whatever's Bothering You
in One Day or Less*

Carol Orsborn

Crown Trade Paperbacks
New York

Published by Crown Trade Paperbacks, 201 East 50th Street, New York, New York 10022. Member of the Crown Publishing Group.

Originally published in hardcover by Harmony Books, a division of Crown Publishers, Inc., in 1995.

Random House, Inc. New York, Toronto, London, Sydney, Auckland

http://www.randomhouse.com/

Crown Trade Paperbacks and colophon are trademarks of Crown Publishers, Inc.

Printed in the United States of America

Library of Congress Cataloging-in-Publication Data
Orsborn, Carol.
    Solved by sunset : the right-brain way to resolve whatever's bothering you in one day or less / Carol Orsborn.—1st ed.
    Includes bibliographical references.
    1. Problem solving.   2. Self-actualization (Psychology).
I. Title.
BF449.O77   1995
153.4'3—dc20   95-24210
                                                          CIP

ISBN 0-517-88779-7

10 9 8 7 6 5 4 3 2 1

First Paperback Edition

Dedication

I dedicate this book lovingly to my husband, Dan—the best fellow traveler one could wish for in life

To my son, Grant—whose perceptive mind often understands my biggest ideas before and better than I do myself

To my daughter, Jody—for her ebullient spirit that too often tempted me to play instead of write this book—but I got it done, anyway

Acknowledgments

With heartfelt gratitude and respect to:
Patti Breitman, my agent and friend, with great affection

Shaye Areheart, my visionary editor

Dean Joseph Hough, Professor David Buttrick,
Dr. Pat Rettew, and my colleagues at Vanderbilt Divinity School

Dr. Lloyd and Mae Matzkin, for loving me always

Contents

✳

How the
Solved by Sunset
Process Works

There is a reason that the problem you would like to resolve by sunset tonight has come to the forefront of your attention at this time. You have been struggling with this issue—and chances are you are feeling some pain about it. But it is a good sign that you reached for this book just now. It is a sign that you are ready to tell the whole truth about the situation you find yourself in—to confront, transform, and transcend old ways of approaching your problems. You want to see them in a new light where they can be resolved once and for all.

I know this process can work for you and that your problems can be resolved satisfactorily, because this is an orderly universe. It supports your evolution unconditionally, regardless of how you feel about yourself or your situation right now.

By applying the *Solved by Sunset* process to the issue that is confronting you today, you will be in exactly the right time and the right place to initiate a new period of resolution and growth in your life. Not only will you receive the expanded clarity and insight you need to best resolve your problem, but you will mature spiritually as a result.

Solved by Sunset is a self-guided process. Ideally, you should set aside one day out of your busy life when you can be left alone to read the book and do the steps as they lead you to resolution. Depending on your geographical location and the time of year, you can probably begin your day at seven or eight A.M. and still finish in time for sunset.

Alternately, you can read *Solved by Sunset* through first and then use the handy guide at the back of the book later, when you have time to dedicate to doing the various exercises.

However you choose to approach this book, think of your time with these pages as your personal retreat. If you have the means, you can certainly make this a particularly special experience by finding a resort or a retreat where you can spend unstructured time either alone or with a group that has gathered with the intention of doing the *Solved by Sunset* process together.

The only tools you will absolutely need are paper and pen. However, you will periodically have opportunities throughout the day to draw on other resources, such as your favorite music and divinatory tools (for example, the Rider-Waite version of the tarot card deck, if you have them or would like to obtain them). A fireplace and a candle might also come in handy.

The only mental preparation you need is to have a problem or issue on your mind—and the fervent desire to resolve it by sunset.

Introduction

Three years ago, my husband Dan seriously proposed that we move our family from San Francisco to Nashville. We were faced with a life-changing decision. But this was nothing new. Dan had also seriously proposed that we make the move four years, ten years, and fifteen years ago. It made sense for us to stay in California —that was where our business, our family, our friends, our *life* was. But Nashville, with its promise of music industry jobs, tugged at his heart—and he, at mine.

Each time the issue emerged, we worked it over, balancing the pros and the cons. We made lists, weighed the odds, talked it out with friends and looked to experts for guidance. We grabbed opportunities as best we could out of our busy lives to puzzle over the possibilities, research alternatives, analyze, and theorize. In other words, we were using the same left-brain rational process we had applied successfully to many of our life issues: from choosing a roofer to renaming our company. We were used to being in control: gathering the information, evaluating the possibilities, and taking decisive action. When it came to the subject of Nashville, however, we were stuck.

Truth be told, this wasn't the only issue that had defied our persistent efforts to call the shots over the years. There were quite a few unresolved issues rattling around just beneath the surface of our busy lives like annoying psychic pets, scratching at the cage door of our rational processes, not quite powerful enough to break the latch but too noisy to be ignored. Some were smaller—the kind of everyday issues related to family, career, love, and life that persistently seem to take up more space and time than you know, down deep, they're worth. Some were bigger—choices swept to the surface by the turbulent changes a fully lived life brings in its wake: decisions related to various stages of the life-cycle, for instance, or brought on by circumstances beyond our control. Every aspect of all our lives is in constant motion and each shift brings with it new questions. If I do this, will it be progress or regression? Is it worth the risk? Stay or go? Yes or no?

This is all well and fine if your routine problem-solving processes can bear the load. But what about those times when you've brought all of your resources to bear on the issue at hand, and you are left uncertain, reactive and fearful? You don't get a say about whether or not your life will present you with challenges, crises, and issues begging for resolution. You know that if you do nothing, the tides of your life will move you when and where they will. But by being willing to act, you will have the opportunity to be an agent of change, rather than its victim. The decision you make, regardless of how you arrive at it, will be the vehicle that moves you forward in your life. *Wouldn't you like to find a satisfying and peaceful resolution to whatever issue is bugging you right now?*

And so it was that three years ago, we once again took up the question of whether to move to Tennessee. What was different this time, however, was that we had developed a new process with which to approach the question—a strategy that bypassed all the loopy left-brain dead ends that had kept us in limbo on this issue for nearly two decades. It was a process that held the promise of breakthroughs, sudden realizations, and expanded perspective, not only resolving the issue that was begging for attention at that moment, but one that held the potential to reorder the fabric of our mental and spiritual consciousness.

After years and years of working over this core life issue, one day we knew that we had the means to resolve it by the end of that very day. And now, three years later, having taught these techniques to thousands of individuals across the country, many of whom have reported similar breakthroughs by applying this approach to issues that are on their minds and in their hearts—I am eager to teach the process to you.

Before I do, however, I need to address the fact that this process is built upon the foundation of three key assumptions that I am going to be asking you to buy into, and that I will be sharing with you presently.

So, let's take a big breath and prepare to jump deeply into the core of the belief system within which *Solved by Sunset* operates. I am inspired here, as I will be periodically throughout this book, by the words of the philosopher William James, whose classic works on human nature pioneered the exploration of the mental and spiritual states that accompany such phenomena as mysticism, conversion, and personal religious experience. At the turn of the century, James wrote of the belief that "there is an unseen order, and that our supreme good lies in harmoniously adjusting ourselves hereto."

While James, addressing an audience at the University of Edinburgh, was speaking primarily of his own Judeo-Christian tradition, his description works well when applied to Eastern philosophy and

Indian mysticism. *The I Ching,* the three-thousand-year-old book of ancient Chinese wisdom that inspired my last work *How Would Confucius Ask for a Raise?,* teaches similarly that there is a hidden archetype of order, known as the Tao, to which the "superior" person aligns him or herself.

"Natural occurrences are uniformly subject to law," explains Richard Wilhelm in his commentary on *The I Ching:*

> Contemplation of the divine meaning underlying the workings of the universe gives to the man who is called upon to influence others the means of producing like effects. . . . It enables them to apprehend the mysterious and divine laws of life, and by means of profoundest inner concentration they give expression to these laws in their own persons.

There is a wonderful story from East Indian folk tradition that illustrates this point. A rainmaker had been invited to a village that had been suffering from drought. When the rainmaker arrived, he asked to be put up in a shack on the outskirts of the village. He would need several weeks of fasting and meditation in order to get himself prepared for the rainmaking ritual. Halfway through his stay, the clouds began to gather and then it rained. The people of the village rushed to his cottage to celebrate with the rainmaker. But he was as surprised as they were.

He said that he hadn't been feeling right with himself—he'd been out of sorts. So he had been spending his time in isolation trying to regain his balance and vitality. He hadn't performed the ceremony yet, and still, through the very act of his sorting things out for himself internally, the rains had come.

Any one of us can stumble into an experience such as this at any time. For example, I received a call several weeks ago from Ray, a businessman in a small town in Georgia who owned what used to be the best laundromat in town. A long-time competitor had offered to buy him out for pennies on the dollar. When he refused, the competitor opened an even bigger and better laundromat nearby. By the time Ray called me, he was bitter and depressed. Business was way off. He thought of the competitor as his enemy and wanted my advice about the situation.

As he spoke, I felt my stomach tighten into a knot. I realized that I was experiencing viscerally the rigidity that had taken Ray out of alignment with the unseen order. After batting the issue around with me for some time, Ray admitted that he had always hated the laundromat business and had been thinking about trying to get out for several years. He just couldn't stand the idea of letting his competitor "win," and try as hard as he could, he could find no other potential buyer for his laundromat. I suggested that what he needed to do was mentally and emotionally release his competitor, replacing every negative thought about him with a blessing, then moving on quickly to other more positive matters. By doing so, the energy would begin to move around and through Ray again.

We set an appointment to talk again the following week. Ray called right on schedule. But he told me the purpose of his call was to cancel the appointment. Had I offended him by asking him to look at his own stuff rather than teaching him how to beat his competitor?

Not at all, Ray quickly assured me. As soon as he'd hung up the phone after our last conversation, he felt how far from his own life path he'd inadvertently wandered, vowing to rectify his errors. The next day, he'd bumped into a friend he hadn't seen for quite some time who inquired about the laundromat business. Seems as if his friend had always wanted to run a laundromat and would Ray let him know if he ever wanted to sell it to him?

Abraham Maslow, honored as the father of humanistic psychology, contends that it is our natural state to have this kind of breakthrough experience—not the exception. He calls such a state "peak experience," defined as a "self-validating, self-justifying moment which perceives the greatest values of a being's existence." These values include wholeness, completion, justice, aliveness, richness, simplicity, goodness, uniqueness, effortlessness, playfulness, truth, and self-sufficiency.

"The emotional reaction in the peak experience has a special flavor of wonder, of awe, of reverence, of humility and surrender before the experience as before something great," Maslow writes.

He arrived at this conclusion by studying mentally healthy rather than mentally ill subjects, individuals who he refers to as "self-actualized." Among his findings: whatever keeps us from experiencing our alignment with the universe is accidental, and can be overcome. Unhealthiness, rigidity, and ignorance are correctable problems that can be transcended.

I propose, then, that we adopt these as our three working assumptions:

Assumption Number One: There is an unseen order in the universe.

Assumption Number Two: Our highest good lies in harmoniously adjusting ourselves to this unseen order.

Assumption Number Three: Whatever keeps us from experiencing our alignment with the universe is accidental, and can be overcome.

In Chinese philosophy, these assumptions are captured in part by the concept of Tao, the unifying principle that brings order out of chaos, meaning out of the void, harmony out of discord. Inner awareness, accessible through right-brain intuition—when not obstructed by alienating character traits such as impatience and greed —connects the individual with universal truths, recognizable on a gut level. The system that I have developed sets up the environment in which the process of harmoniously adjusting yourself to the unseen order will be *most* likely to transpire. (Setting up the environment is the best we can do, because as you will learn shortly, reestablishing your alignment with this unseen order is not something you can make happen—it is something you can only let happen. Happily, this is enough.)

You will discover in the coming pages that much of the latest research in cerebral functioning—particularly as it relates to the neurological roles of the right- and left-brain hemispheres of our brains —supports what *The I Ching* was teaching three thousand years ago, what William James voiced at the turn of the century, what contemporary historians and theologians are pointing to as the wave of the future and what psychologists and spiritual seekers are putting into practice today.

What this harmonious adjustment represents is no less than a completely new way of perceiving the world. It is a shift that takes place on both the intensely personal level as well as on the level of culture and society. In order to set the stage for the process of problem-solving that I will be teaching to you, let us begin by considering the shift that is taking place historically and culturally.

Professor David Buttrick of Vanderbilt University's Divinity School explains that "we live in the midst of a cultural breakdown not dissimilar to the collapse of the Greco-Roman world." The Age of Enlightenment, characterized by "objective reason, individual focus, and an entrepreneurial spirit" is widely considered by contemporary scholarship to have failed, leaving in its wake an intellectual and spiritual void.

This void stems from the breakdown of the illusion that we could control nature and fate through the mental acumen of our rational processes. The illusion was fueled by the ebullient perception that scientific achievements in the past century had made it possible for us to exert an unprecedented influence on external phenomena. As a result of the scientific method, we learned that we could fend off darkness with electric lights and tame bacteria with antibiotics. The very moment of life's initiation has been captured on video as a microscopic camera films sperm struggling upstream in a woman's body, to be shown later that night on the evening news; skeletons uncovered from ancient glaciers fill in the gaps concerning our species' history; and bits of the moon help us understand the nature of the cosmos. We have been tempted to see ourselves as masters of the universe, replacing the need for faith with the promise of scientific knowledge and progress as the means of making peace with the unknown.

The impact of all this scientific knowledge has been that our rational left-brain function—metaphor for the part of our mind that deals mainly with language, logic, and time—has become more highly regarded than our right-brain capabilities—the aspect that specializes in spiritual, intuitive, and spatial orientations. We became overreliant in the direction of the rational, leading us to the false notion that we could have ultimate control over ourselves, our lives, and our situations. We have been led to believe that we can solve all of our problems by working harder, thinking smarter, and perfecting our logic. When something goes wrong, as inevitably it will, we only know how to do more of what was already not working for us: a condition that ultimately leads into the imploding spiral of stress and burnout and the subsequent disruption and exhaustion of our selves and our institutions.

Alternately, Eastern philosophy teaches us the concept of balance that mental, physical, and spiritual health depend on the dynamic interplay of opposites: giving *and* receiving, activity *and* rest, rationality *and* faith, and so on. Every individual has opposing forces within him or her—as does our culture, as a whole. In fact, any entity can benefit from a pure expression of either of those forces at any given moment.

But overall, over time, it is the dynamic tension between opposites that creates true power. *The I Ching* teaches that there is a place within each of us where the forces of action and receptivity, will and surrender, are in proper balance and one experiences true power. The ancient Chinese visualized this process as a pot of water cooking over an open fire. If the fire is too low, the water will not boil. If it's too hot, the water boils away. Only when the balance of forces is just right will the water be capable of doing the work it was intended to do.

In the area of problem-solving, we have all but boiled the very juice out of our left-brain rational systems. For fifteen years Dan and I responded to his urge to move us to Nashville: we worked it over, made lists, weighed the odds, talked it out with friends, and puzzled over the possibilities. Until three years ago, the one thing we had never tried was to shift the issue into a whole new context where not only would we not overwork those poor, tired rational approaches yet again, but where we would actually short out the circuits.

In the void, this shift can take place instantaneously, perhaps not on the societal level, but certainly on the personal: the inner terrain of individual consciousness where your problems and issues are actually experienced, and where breakthrough solutions are possible. Ironically we simultaneously find descriptions for this inner experience in both the oldest and newest understandings of human nature. Looking back through the centuries, before the Age of Enlightenment and the rise of rationalism, there was, in the history of religions, a concept that captures this inner experience's spirit. It's called "inspiration."

Religious scholars, in *The Encyclopedia of Religion,* define inspiration as "a spiritual influence that occurs spontaneously and renders a person capable of thinking, speaking, or acting in ways that transcend ordinary human capacities."

Archimedes had such an experience when, having exhausted his left-brain mental capacities working out the principle of specific gravity, he gave himself a break by taking a bath. As he stepped into the tub, he noticed that the water level rose. This experiential clue provided the breakthrough solution he had been seeking. As the story goes, he shot out of the bath and ran stark naked down the streets of ancient Greece shouting, "Eureka!" (I've found it!)

Carl Jung, confused and upset about his break with his mentor Sigmund Freud, retreated to his family home to lick his wounds. While there, he found himself on the floor playing children's games. Soon he took his childhood fantasies out into the backyard, building out of stone the villages, towns, and forts he'd imagined as a young boy. Spontaneously, he was overtaken by the realizations that form the basis of Jungian psychology.

More recently, writer Anna Quindlen had what she called an "epiphany" while taking a long walk alone in the countryside near her home. Suddenly, after a protracted period of uncertainty concerning her career, it became apparent to her that there was nothing holding her back from quitting her prestigious job as a columnist and deputy metropolitan editor at the *New York Times,* in order to devote her creative energies to writing fiction. She gave up her fast-track career in New York City and began her new career as a novelist, working out of her home.

There seems to be a connection between breakthroughs such as these and the relinquishment of individual will. You stop trying to make things happen, controlling and manipulating external reality—and make room to receive. Call it inspiration or creativity, problem-solving or miracle: the relinquishment of old rational processes creates an increased opportunity for forces beyond your comprehension to become engaged in your success.

The Chinese character for Tao, the depiction of a foot guided by a head, captures the essence of this relationship between forces. The foot represents the rational, intellectual capabilities that relate to the left-brain functions of the cerebral cortex. The head represents intuition and inner wisdom, receptive capabilities that reflect the right brain's contribution. It takes both qualities to comprise the Tao— and they must be in healthy balance. But it is important to note that progress depends on the head leading the foot: we must honor our intuition, our inner knowing, even above our rational, intellectual capabilities.

For years, this irrational category of language was primarily the purview of saints, gurus, and mystics. Happily, in the 1970s, psychologists and neurological researchers began to take the phenomenon seriously. Scientist Roland Fischer, describing the activity of the sympathetic nervous system, dignified the ecstatic mystical state associated with such breakthrough phenomena as "ergotropic arousal." The contribution that science is making to our understanding of the problem-solving process will be explored in the first chapter of this book.

Where science, psychology, and spirituality converge is where the *Solved by Sunset* process begins. Where it leads is to a new understanding of the role of problems in your life, what it means to "solve" your issues, and what it feels like to make the shift to a new way of being. By using the problem that is foremost on your mind right now as a vehicle of transformation, you will gain access to the unseen forces that are operating in your life. You will consider spiritual issues pertaining to your relationship to success, goal-setting, victimhood versus empowerment, faith, acceptance, surrender . . . and more. In fact, this process is so important and meaningful for your life overall, that I suggest you will begin to see the problem you are facing today as the very vehicle of spiritual growth and transformation in all areas of your life, with resolution of this particular issue merely your most likely by-product.

My goal in *Solved by Sunset* is not only to solve your problem by sunset—but to allow you to harmoniously adjust to the unseen order. You can think of this unseen order as the universal life force, as Tao, as your higher self, or as God. However you refer to the unseen order, you are a link in a chain that finds both its roots and its destiny in mystery. You are entrusted in this particular time and place with a sacred task: to bring yourself into alignment with the vital energy of the divine. This is your natural state, a condition that arises effortlessly when you clear away the illusions and fears that clog the channels, letting your vitality manifest with clarity and decisiveness.

So what did Dan and I decide? After listening to ourselves mull ad nauseum the pros and cons and ins and outs of moving versus staying, we decided to take a day out of our lives and use the material from the process I will be teaching you in this book. In short, we decided to drive out to a favorite inn in the country.

On the way, we found ourselves driving on a particularly boring stretch of road. We passed a road sign. We passed a cow. And then, for seemingly no particular reason at all, I had the answer that was fifteen years in coming.

"Why not give Nashville a try?"

Why not give Solved by Sunset *a try?*

Carol Orsborn

Nashville, Tennessee

January 1995

It is the infinite for which we hunger, and we ride gladly on every little wave that promises to bear us toward it.

—*Havelock Ellis*

Setting
Your
Intention

One

The Science of Miracles

Baron Wen Chi, a contemporary of Confucius, said that he always thought three times before he acted. When Confucius heard this, he remarked, "To think twice is quite enough."

Wouldn't you like to solve whatever's most bothering you by sunset tonight? Do you think it would take a miracle?

Give yourself this day—one day out of your busy life—and I can teach you about miracles.

What is a miracle? A miracle is an unexpected occurrence that comes to you from outside your existing expectations and experiences. It is not rational. It is not predictable. It is beyond your control.

I can't teach you how to make a miracle happen—but I can teach you how to create the environment in which miracles are most likely to occur. To do so, you will need to relinquish your routine ways of handling your problems and take a leap of faith to a whole new approach. This new approach is the *Solved by Sunset* process, a series of techniques, exercises, and tools you lead yourself through at your own pace, at your own time, and in your own way. Many individuals who have followed the processes described in this book experience breakthroughs, expanded perspective, and resolution—on both an inner and outer level. Some achieve this breakthrough as a climax at the end of the day's work; others find that answers flood into them just by reading the book—before they've even begun to carry out the processes described in these pages. For these people, the act of setting an appropriate intention, suspending their own personal will, and opening to receive inspiration from unseen forces brings spontaneous resolution. In other words, they are allowing their emotions, psyches, and spirits to be aligned with the unwritten laws of the universe.

This is not a new notion. In fact, at the turn of the century, there was a school of academics—scientists, psychologists, theologians, and philosophers—who created a theory that informs our understanding of such phenomena even today. Their concept of the role of inspiration in problem-solving and resolution is uncannily close to the way contemporary scientists describe the neurological systems involved in the creative problem-solving process.

In 1902, philosopher William James wrote, in his classic work *The Varieties of Religious Experience:*

> A mind is a system of ideas, each with the excitement it arouses, and with tendencies impulsive and inhibitive, which mutually check or reinforce one another. The collection of ideas alters by subtraction or by addition in the course of experience, and the tendencies alter as the organism gets more aged. . . . A new perception, a sudden emotional shock, or an occasion which lays bare the organic alteration, will make the whole fabric fall together.

James's contemporary, Professor E. D. Starbuck, conceived of all sudden breakthroughs of inspiration, insight, and resolution as being akin to the sudden appearance of the tip of an iceberg: new thoughts, ideas, and information that erupt into our consciousness have been gradually incorporated, on an *unconscious* level, developing sufficient strength to burst through to our everyday minds. We experience this moment of clarity as a breakthrough. Suddenly we have insight and enhanced perspective with which to solve our problems.

The I Ching, the ancient Chinese "Book of Changes" that inspired the philosopher Confucius, found poetic words to express this notion three thousand years ago. According to *The I Ching,* life experience is like water filling up behind the wall of a dam. From the other side of the dam, it can look like absolutely nothing is happening. Then, all it takes is one last drop to cause the pooling water to rise over the top and become a rushing river effortlessly flowing into the next stage of its journey.

This example serves as an illustration as to how many individuals who have used the *Solved by Sunset* model to approach their problems experience sudden breakthroughs during the course of the day. Because they are by and large high-achievement people, who have trouble taking time out of their busy schedules to do the kind of inner work prescribed in this book, they are, in a manner of speaking, overdue for a radical configuration of their thought processes. While their normal, routine minds have been busily taking care of business, their subconscious minds have been faithfully gathering new evidence, data, experiences, and ideas. Perhaps they have even read widely in spiritual and psychological literature and have had many previous experiences in alternate ways of approaching their problems—and yet they are still faced with a problem of resistance.

None of this valuable work has been wasted. All these people need is that one last drop. By taking one day out of your busy life to do the processes in this book, *you* are creating the occasion that will allow for the probability of a breakthrough.

This will not simply add new information into an already over-loaded system—a system that, in all likelihood, is a linear model in which more input results in a bigger organization. Rather, the final episode resulting in the kind of breakthrough we are talking about causes the massive and organic reconfiguring of the system into a whole new constellation of reality.

To delve into this more deeply, we turn to contemporary scientific language. In their book *Religion and the Individual,* psychological researchers Daniel C. Batson, Patricia Schoenrade, and Larry W. Ventis explain that each one of us constructs our perception of reality by classifying and differentiating our experiences. Hierarchically arranged, lesser and subordinate ideas and understandings cluster around more general and abstract organizing principles. Logic— our normal, routine, rational ways of approaching our problems— operates *within* the context of these hierarchies, as presently arranged. The researchers write:

> When we are presented with a problem that requires organizing principles at a higher level of conceptual complexity than we have developed, it will appear to be insoluable. . . . Creativity involves an improvement in one's cognitive organization. . . . This is not a logical transformation. . . . Instead, in creative thought the cognitive structures themselves, the very framework within which reflected, rational, logical thought is possible, are changed.

When Dan and I were operating our public relations agency in San Francisco, I remember one such experience of reconfiguration. After many years of productive partnership with a client—a prominent hotel—the marketing director accused us of running out of fresh ideas. This was around the time of the Iran-Iraq War and business was way down—not only for our client, but for all travel-and-leisure companies based in San Francisco. We felt that the accusation was unfair and unfounded. In fact, it was simply the manifestation of a trend that had been growing for some time. Under the economic strain of the war, not only did we feel our relationship with the client become more pressured, but we witnessed relationships within the hotel becoming more distrustful, as well.

We tried to bring this up for discussion with our client, but instead we were sent back to the drawing board to come up with fresh creative ideas. Taking our staff on a weekend retreat at the hotel, we did everything we could think of to come up with the breakthrough that would help us keep this account. We studied competitors' promotional plans, we researched classic marketing strategies. Toward the end of the day, dry, empty, and exhausted, I left the hotel building to walk through the lovely grounds that surrounded it. Letting my mind drift aimlessly, I was admiring the landscaping, momentarily placing my problem on the back burner. After some time, vaguely aware that the setting sun warned that it was time to submit to our final round of brainstorming, I turned back toward the building instantly feeling dread.

But then, unexpectedly, hard on the heels of this negative wash of emotion, I realized I had spent the whole day—and in fact many of the past weeks and months—trying to solve the wrong problem. My thoughts spontaneously reorganized around a new center. At the heart of the reorganization was a memory of a time some years ago when the public relations industry's leading magazine had written a glowing article about our agency, which discussed our Silver Anvil, the highest award our industry offered. I remember taking that article, crumpling it into a ball, and tossing it in the trash. It had no meaning for me. Something had gone wrong with my life, but I couldn't put my finger on it. Looking around at our offices and home, I had ample evidence of our success. But it all seemed only more space to fill—a yawning, greedy emptiness that demanded that I keep investing my vital energy for *its* sake, rather than my own.

Then, as I hesitated on the garden path that would lead me back to my staff, I suddenly thought of something our business advisor,

Len Gross, had said to us some time ago. Len was a sage "retiree" from the advertising business whom I often turned to at moments when life became particularly dense. The day I'd crumpled up that article, we'd gotten together for a consultation. I had been complaining about one unlucky break or another. "Life isn't fair," I remember moaning, expecting Len's customary flow of inspired words that in the past had helped us fix everything from bookkeeping systems to employee compensation issues. I eagerly awaited his wisdom.

He turned to me, fixed his wise, kind eyes on mine, and said, "So?"

So? I hadn't fully understood what he'd meant then. But the word stuck. Now, apparently, the unfairness of the hotel marketing director's demands was to be the last drop I needed to finally get Len's message. For if Len's assessment was correct, then no matter how hard I tried to please this client, no matter how fast I ran, how cleverly I pushed my brain, I could still never do enough to ensure that we could make this situation work. Life is not fair. But if that were true that meant I was free to call off all the old deals with which I had been running my business. Perhaps this was not a matter of why we couldn't come up with the right creative solution for the hotel—it was, rather, why were we staying in a situation that was so damaging to our spirits? My constellation of thoughts shifted around this new idea—this new center. It was not the category of breakthrough I'd expected—but it was the solution that was called for. We resigned the account the next day.

All along, I had wanted us to do what was best for the agency. The old thoughts centered around the idea that we could do this most effectively and efficiently by pleasing the client. The new center consisted of the more productive thought, "What will nurture our own vitality so that we don't burn ourselves out on unreasonable and disrespectful situations?"

Both classic and contemporary psychology researchers point out that people's cognitive structures vary in degree and quality from individual to individual, as they vary within an individual from one stage of development to another. Growth—the experience of moving toward the fulfillment of one's potential—is the process by which one's less adequate cognitive structures are replaced by structures that offer more flexibility and adaptability. In other words, when you've got a problem, like the issue or situation that is on your mind today, this growth is what is called for.

A problem, then—and in particular, the problem you would like to resolve today—is actually a point of entry into the outer limits of the inner workings of your cognitive systems—exactly the place at which growth and transformation can take place. You may feel pressed to make a decision, perhaps about career, business, or relationship issues. You may have had a problematical situation suddenly thrust upon you—or you may be self-selecting to handle something that's been lurking around for quite some time. You may have a generalized sense of something being not quite right—or a specific choice to make that must be made and made fast. Later in this section, you will have the opportunity to define exactly what your particular entry point into the deeper recesses of your consciousness is. Before we proceed, however, I must warn you that in our culture, it takes far more courage and commitment to be willing to do the inner work that is required to resolve your problem by sunset than many are willing to invest. You don't believe me? Then try this on for size:

Imagine that you are overwhelmed with things to do. (This shouldn't require too much of a stretch.) You've got deadlines to meet. Your children or pets are clamoring for attention. Your significant other is feeling neglected. The house is a mess. You are feeling frazzled and burned-out. And now, you've got one day. *This* day. What do you do with it? Scenario Number One: Put this book down and work like a crazy person from sunrise to sunset trying to get everything done, making everybody happy, and hoping to get everything under control once and for all. Scenario Number Two: Find a quiet spot in your house or, better yet, *away* from home, where you can shut the door, turn off the phone, and do the inner work these processes require of you. Which scenario requires more courage and more commitment—Scenario Number One or Scenario Number Two? Whichever requires the most courage, that's what you should do today.

I'm not being coy here. I am assuming you will recognize that the second scenario, the one in which you take a quiet day for yourself, is the one that will lead you to the resolution you are truly seeking. Otherwise you're getting through just another Band-Aid day slapped on the chaos of a life that is begging for transformation, when what you really need is a reordering of the very fabric of your being.

However, I do believe there are times in our lives that call for action of the "I can make it, I can dig in, I can do what it takes" order. If you're trying to get an A on your final exams, for instance, I don't suggest that you take the day before your tests to explore your unconscious cognitive structures. Each of us has occasions in our lives to which we must rise. The problem comes when we rise to the occasion but forget to come back down again. We get into the habit of pushing through our feelings and fears, trying harder and longer, handling, managing, and doing more. Is this one of those occasions when you must simply put your shoulder to the wheel and push? If you truly don't know, you may use that as the issue you would like to resolve by sunset: the need to clarify whether or not the problem you are facing today would best be handled by the rational, action-oriented strategies you've brought to bear in the past or the far riskier new approach I will be leading you through? But you probably already know the answer. Why do more of what you already know doesn't work for you? It's time to try something new.

Are you ready to "waste" your time, to appear to be falling short of your potential, falling apart, shirking your responsibilities, disappointing others—for just one day?

You're still with me? Good. Because now that I've told you how hard it is, I'm going to let you in on something even more daunting to think about.

If you truly want to solve your problems you have no choice but to proceed. In the words of William James, "There are higher and lower limits of possibility set to each personal life." Only when we are willing to "touch our own upper limit and live in our own highest center of energy" can we hope to fulfill the spiritual potential of our lives. Find the highest possible center—the most sophisticated configuration of your cognitive constellation given who you are at this point in your life—and you will feel whole. Settle for anything less and life loses its vitality, emotions sweep you away, and problems get blown out of proportion. You have to be willing to play the game of life from a place where the fulfillment of your spiritual potential is possible or life becomes flat and hopeless. But take one step toward the growth of your character and spirit, and all things become possible for you.

Two

Blowing the Circuits

*In returning and rest you shall be saved, in quietness
and in trust your strength will come into being.*
—*Isaiah 30:15*

You are a unique, complex, dynamic being. Your inner life is as fascinating as your outer circumstances. Those of us who have been fully focused on success in the world have most often sacrificed the time and space it takes to familiarize ourselves with this vast inner resource. As my first journal writing instructor was fond of saying, "You are like a bowl of vegetable soup—because you have stopped stirring, all the goodies have sunk to the bottom." The exercises I am going to be sharing with you today are like a great big spoon. Dig in and see what surfaces. Both your inspiration and your resistance are to be found deep down, at the bottom of the bowl. Let's say you love carrots but hate onions. Unless you are willing to suffer the occasional onion, you won't get the carrots, either. You must approach your life just as you approach the bowl of soup. You must be willing to take it all.

It is best to approach the processes I am going to introduce you to without any preconceived expectations of what your experience of your inner world may be. If you follow my instructions, right now, regardless of the results you achieve during any particular part of this process, you will be doing exactly what has been called for in your life. At any moment during this process, you may become aware of a new energy, a suddenly expanded perception, a renewed sense of purpose and/or intellectual, spiritual, and emotional break-throughs. But understand that much of what you will be guided through is not easy material with which to work. If at any time you feel exhausted or frustrated, put the material down and pick it up again later. Take a walk. Take a hot bath. If the feelings are not resolved on their own, you can seek help from a friend, a teacher, or a spiritual or psychological counselor who is prepared to assist you in coming to a resolution. When you encounter uncomfortable mate-rial—memories, awarenesses about yourself or your situation—re-member this: To be fully successful, you must first be fully alive.

In order to be fully alive, you will need to develop capacities that have been underutilized in the past. It is these undervalued aspects of yourself that contain the potential to short-circuit your rational processes, allowing your inner wisdom to emerge spontaneously into consciousness. What is this powerful capacity? *The ability to relax.*

Think about your life for a moment. Think of how hard you push and drive. In the martial arts, a punch that taps only this self-willed energy becomes brittle and stiff—easy to deflect. If you watch a Bruce Lee movie, notice how lithe and flexible he is. The secret to power in the martial arts is not to be strong all the time. Rather, the master's arm is kept loose from the time it leaves his side all the way up and out. It is only in the last inch of extension that the power is focused, in a final blast of energy. This is the effective punch—the contrast between relaxation and tension.

When I first learned this technique while pursuing my brown belt in karate some years ago, I realized that my life was all tension: all strength, push, drive, and power. What I was missing was the relaxation, the letting go. There were no dynamics at that point in my life. I had so much more power and potential than I had yet tapped. You can see for yourself how this works when you envision a physical punch. Now imagine the possibilities that may exist for you when you apply the principle of *relaxed* power to your mind.

The principle of dynamic contrast in the martial arts goes back thousands of years. Recent neurophysiological theory and research has uncovered the fact that the brain has two contrasting spheres that are dynamically distinct cerebral hemispheres. Amplifying what I wrote earlier, scientists postulate that the left side of your brain is responsible for logic, language, and linear thought. It is the side of your brain that processes information. When you are trying to figure out how to solve your problem, you are working with the left side of your brain. During the preparation stage of your creative process, you utilize your left brain to make lists, gather information, and work hard to find the solution.

Just as in the example of the punch, where all strength and no relaxation proves to be ineffective, left-brain strategy without right-brain input is inadequate to the creative problem-solving process. Happily, there's a second stage, called the incubation stage. Researchers who have studied and applied the theory of hemisphere specificity to creativity have postulated that during this second stage, the left brain loosens its grip, permitting the less dominant right brain to reorganize the cognitive structures. As we stated earlier, it is this reorganization that results in breakthroughs and expanded perspective. It is this incubation stage that forms the foundation of the *Solved by Sunset* process.

That relaxation can be an important step in the problem-solving process can be illustrated by an example from your own life. Think of a time when you misplaced an important object. You tried to remember where you put it. You thought through all the possibilities. You reran your day over and over again. Did I leave it here? There? Finally, coming up dry, you gave up. You became distracted with other aspects of your life. And then, minutes or hours later, sitting before the fire or washing the dishes, it suddenly came to you. Of course: it's in your coat pocket!

The process I am going to ask you to do shortly will artificially disrupt your left-brain domination in order to insert the dynamics of relaxation that I've been discussing. In the best of all worlds, I'd ask you to meditate for an hour. Through meditation, one is trained to disrupt the left brain's Napoleonesque commands with the blessed relief of nothingness. It is extremely effective. You should meditate. You should get up, as many monks do, every morning at four A.M. and sit for several hours staring at a blank wall. You should do this for years. You should get good at this. It is worth the time and trouble.

However, if like me, you have somehow arrived at the abyss of the problem you would like to solve today, having somehow forgotten to get yourself adequately trained in intense meditation practice, there is something else you can do. Zen tradition has produced an alternate process that can undo your normal cognitive modes—but by working *with* rather than *against* your operative thought processes. Rather than fight against your natural tendencies by asking you to think of nothing, I want you to think of everything. I want you to gorge yourself on your problem. Indulge your mind to its fullest. The process is called "Setting Your Intention." I want you to get lots of paper and something to write with. Go find a place where you can be comfortable for ten minutes. Turn off the phone and shut the door. The next section will tell you how to begin.

✸ Process: *Setting Your Intention*

What is your intention for today? What is the problem or issue that is on your mind and what is it you would truly hope to accomplish? For the next ten minutes, I would like you to write nonstop, never taking the pen off the paper, except to turn the page. Write as fast as you can. Write anything that comes into your mind. Don't lead your thoughts—follow them. For instance, you might start out wanting to find the best way to ask your boss for a raise, then ride these thoughts into tomorrow's grocery shopping list, and end with how concerned you are about your mother's health.

If you are stuck for something to write, write "I am stuck, I am still stuck, this stinks how stuck I am," or whatever comes to mind. If you think this process is stupid, write "This is stupid, I hate this, I ought to be doing something more useful with this time." If you are really stuck, or feel as if you can't get your willful, goal-setting, rational mind out of the way, switch your pen to your less dominant hand. Write about how hard it is to write with your other hand. Write down that thought—that thought—that thought. Let mistakes go uncorrected. Keep writing as fast as you can, nonstop, for the whole ten minutes.

This is a process that holds the potential to bridge your conscious, external desires with the deeper material that can begin to emerge naturally and effortlessly once you begin to move your rational thoughts and processes aside.

✸ Resist the urge to predict where this process will take you.

And now: Begin.

Three

Points of Entry

Carrots or onions? You are stirring, stirring, stirring your bowl of soup. Did the solution to your problem effortlessly float to the surface of your consciousness through this process? Sometimes it does. I remember leading a workshop in which an elderly widower wanted to work on pushing through the fear that was stopping him from living out his life's dream: to sell off his house, buy a boat, and travel through the canals and rivers of Europe for the rest of his life. During this first process, I noticed that tears were rolling down his cheeks. At the end of the ten minutes, he came to the front of the room to share his experience. He'd started writing about how much he wanted to go to Europe, but before long, his girlfriend of several years popped into his mind. Following the thought, he began to write about how much he'd miss her if he were to leave on his big adventure. Wheelchair-bound, it was not feasible for her to join him in his life's dream. Then, suddenly, he found his pen writing the words "I love her. I want to stay with her all my life. I want to marry her. That's my real life dream."

You, too, wanted a carrot. I know that. But did you instead get an onion—something you would rather not face right now but that is nevertheless a point of entry into the inner workings of your cognitive structures? You thought your problem was whether to buy a new Jeep or a used Lexus—and instead you find that you are concerned about whether the look on your boss's face the other day (which you hadn't until now realized you'd noticed) meant your job is on the line.

Or worse, did you get no surprises—did your rational mind stay at the controls, either directing your writing to rework old, tired material over and over again or did it blank you out by refusing to let your right brain out to play? It would not be surprising, although it is disappointing, I'm sure, given our society's negative bias against the freedom of a meandering mind. Our culture distrusts this degree of freedom, labeling it as "fantasy" or "daydreaming," degrading it as unproductive or undisciplined.

This disdain is understandable, given the complexity and focus that so many of our contemporary work functions demand of us, be it operating machinery on the factory floor or performing a surgical procedure. We are expected to be conscious, present, and alert. But there is even a greater deterrent to our ability to let go of our conscious thoughts in order to freely explore our intuition and creativity: the Calvinist ethic. The rational efficiencies of the scientific method that infuses so much of our work life, when compounded by the Calvinist ethic, which contends that one's mind would indulge in its natural degenerative inclinations, abandon God, and descend into depravity if left unchecked, is enough to dampen the spirits of many of us on a daily basis. Calvin's solution was to discourage idleness, daydreaming, and playfulness. The Age of Enlightenment urged us to apply ourselves unreservedly to the mastery of the external environment via the scientific method.

These are ethics that play out today in the contemporary workplace, which honor long, stressed hours as a sign of serious commitment. This may well explain why when you are caught staring out the window in the middle of the workday, your boss assumes you must probably not have enough to do. People who leave at a reasonable time, who take their lunch breaks and vacations, are suspect. Turn your 24-hour-a-day computer off, or refuse to answer your mobile phone after hours, and you may well be passed over for a promotion.

Against this societal bias, it is no wonder that it has taken you so long to be willing to give right-brain thinking a chance. I hope this book will reassure you that, rather than making you less productive and more indulgent, finding a balance between the spheres will actually enhance not only your ability to function in everyday life— but your overall vitality as well.

Remember, even your resistances and imperfections can be a point of entry into the *Solved by Sunset* process. For instance, you may be feeling frustration at this moment because you brought your best to bear on this first exercise, and it doesn't appear to have been enough. You haven't resolved your problem yet? You didn't stumble onto your deeper material? But this realization, too, is an entryway, for it is often through pain that we find the surest way in.

I once walked into a Unity Church to deliver a package for a friend who had just been unexpectedly fired from her job. I was feeling terrible for her when my eyes happened upon a blackboard upon which were scrawled seven of the truest words I've ever read: "A broken heart is an open heart."

We need this kind of reminder. It is a welcome antidote to the misguided heroism of the past several decades. There is a dark side to positive thinking, the consciousness movement, and motivational literature (much of which is more closely aligned to the Calvinist ethic than we may ever have guessed). The notion that we could ever be good enough, smart enough, spiritual enough to get our lives to turn out the way we want them to each and every time is a fallacy. We have been taught to take on the responsibility for our health, the power to create and cure illness. Meditate enough, eat lots of organic food, take enough workshops, "set your intention" well enough, follow your heart with sufficient passion, and your dreams will come true.

But when we believe we have the ability to control what happens to us through our actions, we are trapped in our left *do-it-all/make-it-happen* brain. We become a society of superachievers who believe that if we only try hard enough, we can get it to turn out the way we want once and for all. And for those of us who have had the most success, the seduction is the greatest. Because it always seems that if we can just give a little more—try a little harder, do a little better—we can have it all.

But I am here to tell you that it is restlessness, insecurity, and pain that allow you access to the inner resources where the true experience of success—which you've been working so hard to achieve—can be found. This time, instead of trying to mask the pain with a quick fix, find it within yourself to sit quietly with the complexity and imperfection and don't feel compelled to find superficial resolutions.

At this very moment, there are incredible opportunities for you on the periphery of your horizon, but you cannot see them. Why? Because all of your energy has been focused on keeping yourself on course and charging through the obstacles that come your way, in order to reach the goal you have set for yourself. All your driving ambition has done is limit your field of vision, like blinders on a donkey, forcing you to run over the same worn roads again and again.

John Adams, one of the founders of our country, advised: "The mind must be loose." You must release your grip—if you couldn't during the process itself, then do it now. Who cares how you did on this first exercise? Stop judging your results. Let your thoughts and experiences revel in the truth that this process, this response, this life is quite simply not your show. You can influence and have an impact on the course of your life, certainly you can. But can you control it?

Loosen your grip and old fears may surface, old attachments, questions about who and what you are—how you will be received —how you will do. Will you really solve your problem by sunset? Issues of survival seem to be at stake. You may well find yourself asking: *What happened to the happy person I used to be? Am I digging too deep? Why do I feel so crazy and upset about everything? Am I cracking through to someplace wonderful—or just cracking up? Can I have such mixed-up feelings and still function?*

For a time, you may feel terrified. You may feel hurt over and over again. You may seem to have lost the ability to protect yourself. By opening up, you let in and let out all the pain—but you can't seem to move on. You feel like a teenager again, having feelings run away with you, as you did before you erected your facade, your wall of protection that served you so well for so long. That wall is cracking open now due to the force of your own growth, and it's painful.

And yet, even in the midst of the darkness, there's a small voice inside reminding you that life is not a skill to be mastered, but *an adventure to be lived*. I once heard Scott Peck say that the measure of one's psychological and spiritual health is how many crises you can fit into one life. You are ready for this magnitude of transformation —developing your capacity to take on this level of risk. The fact that you have chosen the problem you did today is evidence that your appetite for change has already expanded. Dig down deep into new levels of power, a power that comes only when you are willing to face your fear and proceed anyway. A true sign that you have progressed in your journey is when you recognize that you would rather have the pain of consciousness than forfeit your authentic experience.

An openness to a greater range of life's experiences, while allowing you to interact with and transform your cognitive structures is
the very essence of creativity. In *Religion and the Individual,* Batson,
Schoenrade, and Ventis write:

> In creativity, the cognitive structures that the individual uses to
> think about the world are changed. This cognitive restructur-
> ing leads to the creation of a new reality for the individual.

The time for you to engage in this level of creativity in relation to
your problem is now. You cannot afford to wait for the circumstances of your life to bring you the experience of success you seek.
You first have to generate the willingness to pay the price of what it
means to be fully alive by opening yourself to a broader band of life
experience.

Someone who was willing to pay the price was Donald Marrs,
who was at the time vice president and creative director for Leo
Burnett Company, one of the largest advertising agencies in the
world. Following the dictates of his inner voice, he left the security
of his career in advertising to pursue his dream of working in the
movie business. He moved from Chicago to Hollywood, selling his
home to fund his transition. His wife, deeply ensconced in their
community, had mixed feelings about his midlife shift. So mixed, in
fact, that their marriage ended in divorce. Hollywood, it turns out,
was not the paradise Donald had expected, either. Having run
through his savings, he ended up imposing on the goodwill of new
friends, wondering if his string of bad luck would ever end. Donald's
is not a pretty story, because in his honest and compelling book,
Executive in Passage, he reveals that the process of growth is not
always as neat and tidy as we would wish. But over and over again,
Donald took the path that held the promise of growth for him.
Eventually, through episode after episode of trial and error, he met a

woman who loved him and appreciated the messy process he was undergoing. At last, Donald put together a new life—not the glamorous Hollywood lifestyle he'd envisioned, but something far more satisfying than the job and life he'd left behind.

In *Executive in Passage,* Donald writes about what it took to establish a new relationship with his life:

> It was as if nature had said, "So you want to change your life? Well, the laws of ultimate reality will let you, but you have to be willing to move into uncharted territory for a while. When you step out of the old, you erase the ironclad laws that once governed you, and for a period of time, you will go without perceivable direction. So here is a warning: in between the time you erase the old laws and before you discover the new, you will experience a void. . . . You will have only your inner star to guide you. But if you persist, and are willing to face any challenge, you will find that it is through the very act of overcoming the challenges and melting the fears that you will replace the old rules with the wisdom needed to create the new life you're looking for."

How often are you willing to follow the dictates of your heart—but only as long as the span of time between taking action and receiving a reward for having done so, is no longer than you find comfortable. When you act in this way, it is as if you are being a fair-weather friend to your inner dictates. You praise God, the universe, and your own goodness—but only if things turn out on schedule, as ordered. But take even the tiniest baby step in the direction of acting authentically—and not get what you want instantly—and you are the first to abandon ship. *Oh,* you say, *I guess listening to my inner voice doesn't work after all. Do you know any good, safe, boring processes I can rush back to, just like the ones I left behind, that may offer temporary relief but leave the core issues essentially untouched?*

Some time ago, I was traveling around the country promoting my latest book. Things were going well enough, giving lectures and interviews. But when I got to Los Angeles, something gave way. Several of the bigger radio shows I had hoped to appear on didn't come through. The daily newspapers passed. I had pinned all my hopes on the booking my publicist had obtained for me on one of the morning television talk shows. Sitting in the green room backstage, my mind drifted back and forth between the plate of doughnuts in front of me, my own internal preparation for the message I planned to deliver, and the news of the moment, which projected off a television monitor in a corner of the small cold room.

When at last the producer's assistant came to fetch me for the bright lights of the studio, I gladly followed her onto the set. Quickly, I was seated beside the host, lapel microphone attached, and introduction rolling. The host turned to me and said, "In your book, you give an example of a meditation technique you can do right at your desk at your job. Can you teach it to me?"

"Of course. What I'd like you to do is find a point of space somewhere in the distance, and soften the focus of your eyes. That's good. Now, breathe in slowly and . . ."

Before I could instruct him to breathe out again, he shot up in a frenzy—the cameras were racing around the studio—the microphone was being ripped off my lapel. What had I done? Was my host having a heart attack?

As it turns out, somewhere in L.A. a horse had fallen into a ditch. The station had managed to get their mini-cam there first. I had been preempted by a fallen horse.

Needless to say, I was upset. I couldn't shake the feeling that if only I had been more effective, if I had a bigger name, a snappier topic, anything, I could have held my own against that horse. What would it have taken to make my message more memorable than a horse in a ditch? I wanted this issue solved before my next interview.

In fact, I wanted it solved by sunset. As I ran and reran the incidents of the morning, I realized that my routine left-brain processes were grinding over old turf to no avail. So, taking a page from my own teachings, I decided to set my problem aside and indulge my right brain for a change.

In short, I decided that I would take my depressed self to spend the evening at Disneyland to witness a much-promoted sound and light extravaganza. Before long, I was sitting on the banks of the Adventureland lagoon, my depression overwhelmed by the drama of a classic cinematic battle between Good and Evil, projected on monstrously huge clouds of mist looming above my head. Illuminated by the glow of fire and lasers. I hadn't felt this humbled before the awesome potential of the universe to surprise and astound since I had witnessed my first fireworks display as a young child. The fallen horse incident seemed long ago, far away—and even, truth be told, a little on the funny side. I caught myself feeling better about myself and the situation.

But then a feeling of sadness unaccountably swept over me: Does it take this much, this many billions of dollars of technology, and the genius of Walt Disney to astound and manipulate, to give me the message that there are larger forces at work in the universe than my own puny efforts to control and manipulate the things that happen to me? There was something in the two encounters—one of pain, one of awe—that reminded me of the humble role I play in the overall scope of things. That morning there had been a horse in a ditch. Now it was celluloid in the mist. Experience is constantly knocking at the door, begging us to put aside the arrogant illusion of power to allow the real adventure to unfold.

A classic story drawn from the Yoga tradition illustrates this point. An Indian mystic wandered from house to house, begging for food and shelter. No one in the village would open their door to this stranger. Eventually, cold and hungry, she walked into the hills outside the village to spend the night. Shivering, she huddled down on a patch of dirt beneath the shelter of a tree. In the coldest hour before dawn, she suddenly awoke—the beam of the full moon bathing her face in light. The tree had burst into bloom and glorious white blossoms were turned toward the lunar illumination. The mystic wept with joy and gratitude, blessing the villagers for turning her away. If it weren't for them, she would have missed the experience of her lifetime: the opening of her heart to the richness of the universe, seeing past the busyness of her efforts to survive for a rare glimpse of the mystery.

As the richness of your inner life becomes as challenging and fascinating as that of your external environment, you will find that attachment to your problems—the idea that your solutions must come in any one way—will dim in importance. It's not that you won't appreciate—and won't sometimes get—easy answers in neat packages. But whether it comes on schedule, as you've ordered it, will no longer be the criteria with which you judge your success. Of course there will be challenges ahead for you—I'm sure you will have moments of regret and discomfort. But if you can see these things as points of entry—ways in—you can begin to experience the resolution that comes when you realize that life itself is a process, not a goal. Have you been postponing the experience of fulfillment until the final results are tallied? If you are hanging around waiting for your solution to make you happy the satisfaction you seek will continue to elude you. There will always be something more you will have to accomplish first.

You can let your goal-orientation go now and replace it with the deeper realization that the authentic urge to follow the "way in" always bears with it a felt sense of rightness that is far more true and dependable than any illusions of success you had ever hoped to achieve out of having, doing, making, and controlling. If you truly want your solutions to bring the fulfillment you long for, then you've got to let yourself be fulfilled by the process of your life first —regardless of what the circumstances surrounding you at any given moment happen to be. With enough discipline and practice, you can learn to feel as if your goal had already been achieved, regardless of external reality. Then, when good things happen to you, they are no longer the criterion for fulfillment, but rather their by-product— that which happens to you along the way while you are living your life.

Old paradigm approaches to problem-solving taught individuals to push through their feelings to achieve their goals. The inner world was devalued as success was defined by levels of external attainment. In this old paradigm, logic, will, and brute force were the primary tools of resolution. Short-term, it often appeared as though one had solved his or her problems and resolved the issue at hand—but more often than not, long-term success proved to be illusory. This is because life is an ever-changing process and not a static achievement.

Those who aim to solve their problems by getting the external manifestation to turn out the way they want are doomed to spend much of their lives frustrated by their inability to get their issues handled once and for all.

The new approach that I am sharing with you teaches problem-solvers to go beyond logic, will, and force to encompass an expanded world of possibilities. In this paradigm, you are being taught to balance the left-brain urge to master and control with the right-brain willingness to surrender to the process of living life fully. You learn to access inner spiritual resources—such as faith, acceptance, patience, creativity, and inspiration—to assume the experience of success you had once thought possible only through external resolution.

Ironically, by letting go of your old way of solving problems, you find yourself with increased perspective. Creativity and intuition are available to be tapped, leading you to breakthrough realizations. Issues that have been with you for years "magically" lose their sting. You can move from the anxiety of fear-driven reactivity to your problems to the certainty of being deeply connected to a process of resolution that offers the experience of success you truly seek.

HOUR
NUMBER
TWO

Bracketing
the
Descent

Four

Feed Your Demons

Though He slay me, yet will I trust in Him;
but I will argue my ways before Him.
—*Job*

In our contemporary understanding of the world, the experience of pain means that you've failed. We are a society that works very hard at protecting ourselves from discomfort. Over-the-counter medications are a multi-billion-dollar industry. Sales of Prozac, the antidepressant drug, are at an all-time high. The person experiencing negative emotions is seen as "troubled." The individual in pain wonders where they've gone wrong.

In the *Solved by Sunset* model, the experience of pain is not perceived as something about you that failed, but rather the vehicle that will carry you into your next highest center. Let us take a moment to refresh ourselves on the three assumptions upon which this book is based:

Assumption Number One: There is an unseen order in the universe.

Assumption Number Two: Your highest good lies in harmoniously adjusting yourself to this unseen order.

Assumption Number Three: Whatever keeps you from experiencing your alignment with the universe is accidental, and can be overcome.

It is the process of overcoming to which we now turn our attention. We have seen in previous chapters that beginning with the turn-of-the-century philosophers and psychologists, modern science has been studying the question of how it is that we expand our capacities to solve our problems. William James characterized this process as one that is apt to bring pain along with it:

> The normal evolution of character chiefly consists in the straightening out and unifying of the inner self. The higher and the lower feelings, the useful and the erring impulses, begin by being a comparative chaos within us—they must end by forming a stable system of functions in right subordination. Unhappiness is apt to characterize the period of order-making and struggle.

Spiritual teachers from many ages, faiths, and perspectives, like James, view pain not as a bad thing to be avoided but as a necessary and important growth step to full spiritual maturity. This spiritual interpretation of pain has many names. Some call it "the void." St. John of the Cross, in the fifteenth century, called it "the dark night of the soul." However you refer to it, one experiences it as the period that comes between what was and what's next. Within its darkness, it has no boundaries and no landmarks. When you are inside it, it feels that there will be no end. Fortunately, there are many "survivors" who have journeyed through the void and emerged more vital, more integrated, more connected to life's possibilities, not despite of, but because of the experience. The void is, after all, perhaps the most effective place for the reordering of one's cognitive processes to take place, for that is where one is least invested in the structures that once circumscribed meaning in one's life.

In the void, ways that were previously employed in the solving of one's problems no longer work. But in the dark night, even this dysfunction, while adding to the pain, can lead to growth. William James teaches us that relief from one's problems is often "a more commonplace happiness." The spiritual state, he knows, is possible for those courageous enough to traverse the void, not looking for superficial resolution or escape, *but for more life.*

The experience James is referring to is echoed in the writings of the Jewish mystics, who call the individual willing to engage in this level of participation a *tzaddik,* a righteous leader. According to the great Hasidic teacher Rabbi Nachman, the true tzaddik is a constant *baal t'shuvah*—a sinless penitent who begs forgiveness for not having attained a higher spiritual level than the one he or she has already reached. Dissatisfaction is the state that lets the tzaddik know when it is time to make a new effort at advancement. To stay at one's current spiritual level, regardless of how exalted it might be, is considered a sin.

I remember in particular one incident that initiated a dark night in my life. Our public relations company had just landed one of the plum accounts in San Francisco—the city's leading shopping complex, Embarcadero Center. We were hot, we were happening, we were on top of the world. The complex opened a new addition —and we commandeered the press as if they were our own foot soldiers: headlines, top of the nightly news, magazine spreads. At the conclusion, I was called to the marketing director's office expecting a bonus and a handshake. Instead, we got a pink slip. Thanks very much, but our services were no longer required.

This does not happen to a master of the universe. But it happened to me. The news sent me reeling. For the first time, I saw the underbelly of my life's mechanistic premise, which had served me well enough to this moment: Work hard and you will be rewarded. The Calvinist ethic. Now, suddenly, I realized that there was a terrible flip side to this message because logically, if I were being rewarded when good things happen, then when something goes wrong it must mean I was being punished.

Where did I go wrong? This is a loaded question, holding to the empty promise that there would always be something I could do— some quality or quantity of behavior—that would control the things that would happen to me. I would rather have kept the notion that this event had to do with some shortcoming on my part than to consider the alternative: that there are limits to my ability to affect reality and that I was bound to suffer unfairly from time to time. *Punish me, if You must, for in punishment is the hope of correction and subsequent reward. But don't make me confront the despair of my own human limitations.* This particular event was so totally unfounded and unjust, however, that my brave attempts to hold on finally gave way and I fell into the void.

Many of the events that transpired in the years following this incident have been detailed in my previous books: how I reevaluated the amount of time and energy I had been investing in my work as opposed to other neglected aspects of my life and relationships (*Enough Is Enough*); how I began to use my company as an experiment, trying out new, more humanistic and spiritual approaches to productivity on myself and my staff (*Inner Excellence*); how I redefined success as having less to do with pushing through feelings and values to achieve a goal and more to do with nurturing the growth of my character and spirit, trusting that my greatest achievements will come as by-products of the process (*How Would Confucius Ask for a Raise?*). Little did I know at the time of our dismissal that out of the desperate experience of grasping the dark night air, I would be subconsciously fashioning a new career, a new perspective about life and my problems, and a new sense of purpose and vitality.

In studying spiritual literature, I have identified five stages that one must pass through in order to traverse the void. I have numbered them, but they are not linear. Each contains all the others, and at any stage, all may be experienced simultaneously. The stages of the dark night of the soul are:

1. The Willingness to Descend

In this first stage, you come to understand that the fact that you have problems resulting in pain, indecision, and vulnerability is not about what's wrong with you, but about what's right. In psychological terms, this phase is known as "preparation," stemming from your inability to solve your problem using your old cognitive structures. Rather than resist the pain, you realize that your emotions are giving you a point of entry into your deeper material, where transformation and breakthroughs are possible. It takes a courageous person to engage in the level of questioning that emerges from the void.

A man who willingly confronted pain in order to grow was Jacob, son of Isaac. I'm sure you remember the story from the Bible about Jacob and his brother Esau: how Jacob used a sheepskin to simulate the hair on his brother's arm in order to steal his brother's blessing from his blind and trusting father. From there, Jacob climbed the ladder of success, continuing to play in the world of deception, taking turns being deceived by others, and defrauding and betraying them right back. By the time he hit midlife, he had acquired a large attractive family, wealth, position, and not just one wife but two. Far away from the scornful memory of his father and Esau, he looked to the world as if he had it all. But there was one thing his clever manipulations had failed to bring him: resolution.

As so often happens in spiritual stories—as well as in our lives, as long as we are asking the right questions and are willing to engage in the real struggles—the yearnings of our heart can be answered. For Jacob, they were answered in a place of deep descent called the Jabbok River. Jacob had packed up his formidable possessions and embarked on what he hoped would be a journey toward reconciliation with his brother. By the time the descent into the river gorge was complete, it was deepest night. Something prompted Jacob to send his caravan across the river into the darkness of the distant shore while he remained behind. No children to distract him. No heads of cattle to count. No wives to entertain. Alone, stripped of his belongings, he was confronted by a spirit who came to wrestle with him. All night long, he struggled with his deceit, his desire to dominate and control, his shame, and his fear in the form of this divine spirit. He struggled with the very imperfection of his own humanity—that painful discrepancy we all feel from time to time between how we hope we are being perceived by others and the flawed versions of reality we fear ourselves to be.

Eventually the sun rose, as it always does. The struggle ended, but not before Jacob understood how much his decision to do whatever it would take to find resolution would cost him. He who for so long had sought only to stride triumphant over others, had engaged in a struggle that left him lame, exhausted, and begging God for a blessing. The important thing is that he was willing to engage in the struggle—he was willing to be broken. It was more important, after all, to face the truth about himself and to make the painful commitment to try to do better, even if that meant he could no longer keep up appearances.

But because Jacob is human, I believe he was forced to wrestle with a second issue that night. He did, after all, receive God's blessing in the end—and went on to meet his brother Esau, who forgave and embraced him. And so perhaps he was guided to forgive himself for his failings as well. This may be the harder lesson to learn. Can you see the whole truth about yourself—your failings and imperfections—and, while vowing sincerely to do better in the future, continue to live with vitality, hope, and commitment knowing full well that because you are human, there will always be a discrepancy between your ideals and your reality?

Jacob's experience reminds us that we may deceive others, make mistakes, and get our values turned around, but when we become willing to take on our emotions at this level of integrity, we are engaging in a struggle worthy of us. You will be forced to grapple with the despair of your own imperfect humanity—and yet choose to live. This initiates the second stage.

2. Unconditional Surrender

Our initial response is to avoid or resist the pain. On the other hand, saints, mystics, and gurus teach us that it is not by *pushing away* but rather by *jumping in* that we find the fastest way through. One becomes willing to experience the pain fully and ask all the questions, trusting that by letting go of the old structures, you are making space for something better to take its place. In psychological terms, this is the stage of incubation—the giving up of your attempt to solve the problem by using ways that worked in the past.

Pema Chodron, director of Gampo Abbey, the first Tibetan monastery in North America established for Westerners, illustrates this point with the story of Milarepa, one of the lineage holders of the Kagyii lineage of Tibetan Buddhism.

Milarepa was a hermit, passing many years alone trying to perfect himself by meditating in the caves of Tibet. One night he returned to his cave after gathering firewood only to discover that demons had taken over his abode. There was a demon reading Milarepa's book, there was one sleeping in his bed. They were all over the place. Hoping to control the situation, Milarepa came up with an idea. He would teach them about spirituality. He found a seat higher than theirs and began to lecture about compassion. The demons simply ignored him. Then he got angry and charged at them. They simply laughed at him. Finally he gave up, sitting down on the floor of the cave with them, surrendering to the fact that since they would not be going away, they might as well learn to live together.

At that moment, they left—all except one. (There is always one—the one you most dread.) Recognizing the need for total surrender,

Milarepa had but one last resort. He walked over and put himself right into the mouth of the demon. He literally fed himself to his demon. At that moment, the demon departed, leaving Milarepa alone but transformed.

3. Demand One's Rights

There comes a moment, if one is watchful, when surrender turns to protest. We have the right to have a relationship with God and the universe that makes sense of our lives. We have the right to fairness, stability, and justice. We do not always get these things.

My friend Melissa called me from San Francisco. She was one of my "workshop buddies," a fellow seeker who delighted in exploring the various ways that individuals through time and in a wide variety of cultures have sought to gain an understanding and experience of the "unseen order." We had taken many classes and seminars together, experiencing bits and pieces of many classic spiritual traditions along with a veritable buffet of psychological, psychic, and inner awareness offerings from contemporary times. We had always prided ourselves on walking the road less traveled.

Melissa and I hadn't spoken for some time, but I knew instantly that she was still dealing with a stubborn problem that had persisted through all of her inner experiences. As always, her intellect danced with spiritual possibilities, but her emotions wrestled with the fact that, at thirty-eight, she had not yet found her soulmate. She was anxious about finding a suitable partner in life, and terribly lonely. Her voice came to me over long-distance from the depth of the abyss. I asked her if she had a Bible in her house. She thought I was kidding. The last thing she thought she needed were reassuring words of comfort and faith. What she wanted was a solution. I asked her to bear with me while turning to the 88th Psalm.

O Lord, God of my salvation,
I have cried day and night before thee;
Let my prayer come before thee: incline thine ear unto my cry;
For my soul is full of troubles: and my life draweth nigh unto the
grave.
I am counted with them that go down into the pit; I am as a man
that hath no strength:
Free among the dead, like the slain that lie in the grave, whom
thou rememberest no more: and they are cut off from thy
hand.
Thou hast laid me in the lowest pit, in darkness, in the deeps . . .

She was waiting for the punchline, the happy resolution at the end. But the 88th Psalm went on for twelve more verses of despondent prose, ending with *"Lover and friend hast thou put far from me, and mine acquaintance into darkness."*

What was my purpose in sharing this with her, then? It was my reminder to her that the feelings of despair she was experiencing were not hers, alone, but belonged to all times and all ages.

The 88th Psalm is the vital spirit asserting itself. One engages in the struggle, demanding the right to make sense of one's relation to the universe. We must take on the willingness to ask the big questions and feel the big emotions, regardless of where our questions may lead. The English writer and critic Katherine Mansfield, who died in 1923, wrote in her journal:

There is no limit to human suffering. When one thinks: "Now I have touched the bottom of the sea—now I can go no deeper," one goes deeper. And so it is for ever . . . I do not want to die without leaving a record of my belief that suffering can be overcome. For I do believe it. What must one do? There is no question of what is called "passing beyond it." This is false.

One must submit. Do not resist. Take it. Be overwhelmed.
Accept it fully. Make it part of life. . . . The present agony will
pass—if it doesn't kill.

Psalm 88 got Melissa's attention. Soon thereafter she asked me to
send her an early draft of this book, so that she could try out the
processes on her own stubborn problem. When she got to the exercise I'm going to lead you through next, she had a major breakthrough. But before I tell you more about her experience, I want
you to do the exercise on your own.

One final thought before you continue your own descent. Joseph
Campbell, in conversation with Michael Toms of New Dimensions
Radio, shared the fact that he was particularly taken with a quote
from *La Queste del Sainte Graal,* the Grail story. King Arthur's knights
were seated at his table, but Arthur would not let the meal be served
until an adventure had occurred. Sure enough, something wonderful
happened. The Grail appeared to them, carried by angelic powers,
veiled by a cloth. Then, abruptly, it disappeared. Arthur's nephew
Gawain proposed that the Knights pursue the Grail in order to see it
unveiled. And so they set off.

The lines that so moved Campbell were these: "They thought it
would be a disgrace to go forth in a group. Each entered the forest
that he had chosen where there was no path and where it was
darkest."

Campbell continued: "Now, if there's a way or a path, it's someone else's way. . . . What is unknown is the fulfillment of your own
unique life, the likes of which has never existed on the earth. And
you are the only one who can do it. People can give you clues how
to fall down and how to stand up, but when to fall and when to
stand, and when you are falling, and when you are standing, this
only you can know."

This next process points to something even greater than the road
less traveled. It points to the way that has no road at all.

At this point, I will temporarily interrupt the five stages so that you may undertake the second hour's process. We will complete our discussion of the five stages when you return.

✳ Process: *Bracketing the Descent*

During this second hour, your only assignment is to experience your emotions fully. Put some evocative music on your stereo. If you've got a fireplace, throw on a log. Shut the doors so that you will have total privacy. And let yourself go as deeply into your feelings as you are able. Don't write. Don't read. Don't do anything but feel.

If you are angry, try beating on pillows. If you are sad, keep plenty of tissues nearby. If you have trouble feeling your emotions, get angry about that! Each time an emotion comes up, try to name it. The Tibetan Buddhists have a practice in which they see Buddha in everything. When you are fearful, that is fearful Buddha. When you are anxious, that is anxious Buddha. When you are angry, that is angry Buddha. When you feel nothing, that is nothing Buddha. Keep stirring the pot. Sooner or later, something is bound to rise to the surface. It is time to stop zigzagging around the sore spots: time to go right through where it hurts most. Let yourself fall apart.

Maybe you think you do this all the time. That this assignment will be easy for you. You are always anxious or angry or something. But what it is you always do is let only the shadows of those emotions rise to the surface—little wheezes and sniffles, depressed little gasps. Only as much emotion as you know you can safely control.

What is called for here is to exhaust your emotions.

But if you let yourself fall apart, will you ever get it back together? You know you've been holding your act together with safety pins.

What if you should disassemble, disappearing into the dark night of the soul never to emerge again? How will you ever solve your problems by sunset?

Here's how. You are going to bracket your descent. For the purposes of the process I am leading you through, you are going to give yourself one full hour to indulge your emotions. Set aside the time for this process, giving it a distinct beginning and a distinct end. Set an alarm clock if you are fearful that without a reminder you will disappear into the void. This hour is all for you. Don't judge the process or your progress. Simply spend this time with one goal in mind: to be as authentic as you are able. At the end of this hour, we will proceed together to the next step. The time to begin is now.

Five

Can You Trust
Your Emotions?

Any attempt to make a good impression, a favorable appearance—
will instantly vitiate the effect. But speak the truth, and all things
alive or brute are vouchers, and the very roots of the grass
underground there do seem to stir and move to bear your witness.

—*Ralph Waldo Emerson*

So it is that when you express your true emotions, the universe
can seem to shift on its axis. It is possible to have a breakthrough
on the problem you have chosen to address today through the process
you just experienced. In a moment I will share with you Melissa's resolution—along with several other accounts of transformation
that emerged from this process.

But before I do, we must address several key issues that may have
come up for you during this past hour: Can you trust your emotions?
Can you differentiate your truth from your theatrics? How do you
know for sure what you are truly feeling? What does it mean to be
authentic?

In the earlier chapters of this book, you may recall my discussion concerning the Eastern approach to breaking the rational left-brain circuits: emptying one's thoughts through meditation. Instead I proposed that you go to the other extreme: overload the circuits by indulging your thoughts rather than attempting to quell them.

The same extremes present themselves to us in relation to our emotions. In Eastern philosophy, emotions are considered the product of reason. As you will recall, our rational processes develop and operate through comparison. Eastern philosophy places the source of all negative emotion in this duality of comparison. I am unhappy *because* there is something I would prefer. I am angry *because* I wanted things to turn out one way but they are turning out another. I am ashamed *because* I know I should act in this way, but instead I acted in that way.

If there were no comparison, there would be no negative emotion. What you would be left with, should you be successful in quelling the dissonance, would be the essential experience itself. It is the experience of "being in the present," where you surrender to whatever's happening without judgment.

The quintessential story that illustrates this point is that of a Zen monk who lived near a village in Japan. A young woman in the village had a child out of wedlock. When her parents pressed to know who the father was, the mother falsely accused the monk. The parents brought the baby to the monk and demanded that he raise the child. His response: "Ah, so?" He lovingly cared for the child for several years. The child was quite beautiful and brought great joy to the monk as well as to the villagers. When the child's mother saw how special this child was, she regretted having given the child away. So, at last, she told her parents the truth about who the real father was. Her parents came to the monk's door and led the child away to their home, never to return. The monk's response: "Ah, so."

As difficult as this level of surrender is to imagine—let alone practice—its value is illustrated by an experience that was recently related to me by a friend who is an inspirational speaker. David was asked to give a talk before a group of defense industry executives on the subject of "Motivating Employees from the Inside Out." The talk, based loosely on my books, was scheduled for 3:30 in the afternoon. David knew that the company had been going through radical downsizing—their work force had been cut from 4,000 to 1,700 over the past several years. Despite knowing that there was a lot of pain in that room, David did not edit his thoughts for his talk: "You want to inspire your employees? First you must ask yourself, are you inspired yourself? Are you willing to do the deep inner work of finding out what your authentic experience truly is?" David spoke about the fact that many companies slap motivation programs like Band-Aids over cultures that are full of distrust and unhealthy competition.

"Companies working on morale issues demand that their workers go play pool together after work in order to have a bonding experience, when the employees would much rather be at home with their families."

By the time David finished, the room was in a dead silence. He asked for questions or comments. There were none. What had gone wrong? He'd given a talk that he instinctively felt would have an impact on his audience. Yet his emotions were telling him in no uncertain terms that he'd failed. The degree to which David was trusting his emotions as being authentic was the degree to which he was seriously considering whether he ever wanted to go before a business audience again.

But David soon realized that you can't always trust your emotions to tell you the truth about reality because at the conclusion, feedback forms were collected from the attendees. The comments were overwhelmingly positive. David's intuition had been right on—but why had his fear seemed so justified? The answer to his question came scribbled on one of the comment sheets:

"What you said was so true and so painful, I was speechless. Did you know that our workday goes from 7:30 A.M. to 3:30 P.M.? We were asked to stay late for this."

The human resource people who had set up this day were moved by David's insights and, subsequent to his talk, took a step in the right direction. The least they could do, they realized, was to initiate workshops and bonding sessions within the workday—going so far as to hire temps and reduce workloads on those days so that managers would no longer be inadvertently punished when the true intention was to motivate.

In the West, we so often experience our feelings as if they were actual reality. Zen teaches that this confusion is caused by the fact that our intuitions (our authentic experience of reality) and our emotions (our desire-based reaction to our experience of reality) travel the same neurological channels. The key way you can tell the difference is that intuition accepts and responds to what is—the "ah, so" experience—while emotions contain desire, the wish to have things be different (or if they are pleasant, to keep things as they are.)

If we in the West did have the capability of quelling our emotions, perhaps that would be the most effective way to clear the neurological channels of confusion, allowing our natural knowing to flow freely. However, just as I suggested that we not yet try to tackle emptying our minds, so it is I propose an alternate way to handle our emotions.

William James explains that there are two ways in which it is possible to get rid of anger, worry, fear, despair and so on: "One is that an opposite affection should overpoweringly break over us and the other is by getting so exhausted with the struggle that we have to stop."

As I've written earlier, we can't make "the opposite affection" break over us. We can only create an environment in which such breakthroughs can transpire. If we can't quell our emotions by transcending the duality of desire, we can, at the very least, exhaust ourselves with the struggle. We can begin by learning to say "Ah, so" to our emotions.

I promised earlier to tell you what happened to Melissa. Now is the time. During the hour of her process, Melissa had begun by wallowing in self-pity, guilt, and shame. She felt that her single state was obviously due to her failings as a human being. If only she were more attractive, had a better personality, had chosen to live in a city with more available men. Over and over again, she ran through her list of inadequacies, shortcomings, and failures, equating the emotions they carried with the truth of external reality.

Then she remembered the 88th Psalm. But this time, she realized something she hadn't before. As despondent as the words and emotions of that psalm were, the author was sharing those dark sentiments within the context of faith. This was a faith so strong that it could express anger and despondency, and know that even these darker emotions would be embraced by the divine. Riding the crest of this notion, Melissa understood that the only demon she had left in her cave was her reluctance to express her anger and to proclaim her right to ask for justice from the universe. At that moment, rather than seeing the problem as "How can I fix what's wrong with me?" she suddenly began to see her issue as much bigger than her own individual experience. She realized that her issue was, in truth, *"How does an imperfect human being make peace with an imperfect world?"*

I heard from Melissa several weeks later. Inspired by the fact that I had at the age of forty-six embarked on the pursuit of my Masters of Theological Studies degree at Vanderbilt University's Divinity School, she had decided to go back to school as well. She was deciding among psychology, philosophy, and religion.

Not surprisingly, several months later, she dropped me a note to let me know she had enrolled in a graduate program in psychology. In passing, she mentioned that she had become quite close to one of her fellow students and was feeling a whole lot better about herself and her prospects. Her crisis of despair and uncertainty had passed.

And so, with this degree of trust in mind, we are ready to continue our consideration of the five stages of traversing the void.

4. Transfiguration

Transfiguration can occur whether or not your objective/external reality appears at the time to have been altered. In psychological terms, this is the stage following preparation and incubation called "illumination"—the emergence of a new cognitive organization that allows the individual to perceive the various aspects of any particular problem in a new light, permitting resolution. In Melissa's case, illumination manifested in several stages; one several weeks later when she decided to go back to school, another several months later when she began to feel close to one of her classmates. Like a pebble thrown into a pond, the ripple effects of the shift to a higher center can continue on for years.

The effects of this shift are sometimes dramatic, as in the case of Melissa. But sometimes, as in the personal story I am about to share with you, it is much subtler. Several weeks ago, I felt besieged by problems. I had a major paper due at school; my children had various situations arise requiring my immediate attention; I had an important decision to make in relation to the marketing of one of my books; and I received bad news about the health of a close relative. On top of it all, I couldn't get the attention or support from Dan that I would have liked because he was up against his own project deadlines. Angry at everybody and everything, I slammed the front door and tromped the hill to my favorite place of refuge: Radnor Lake. Radnor is cousin to Walden Pond, an oasis of nature in the middle of Nashville, one block from my home. On this evening, the stormy weather was a match for my mood. Cold, bitter rain scratched at my face. The trees bent menacingly toward me in the wind, howling so loud it would have been impossible for anyone to hear my angry screams, had anybody else been foolish enough to be out on such an evening. I felt so hopeless, I couldn't imagine any new input, new insights, new thoughts ever offering me relief.

And so it was, at this moment of darkest night, that I accepted that the problems I was facing were not going to magically disappear —that I was not calling the shots in this situation—and that I had the right to be angry and upset. Suddenly I understood that I had been thinking that it was my job to be stable and cheerful—to help my family members out with their difficulties and not to impose my own problems on them. I had been acting a role that had been squashing my right to be authentic and whole. Now I realized that *I had the right to be authentically and wholly upset.* As the wind whipped around me, this new, exciting thought gave me permission to let myself have negative feelings. I was not in control of my circumstances and I had the right to be upset about it.

The fourteenth-century Christian mystic Meister Eckhart, describing how it is that illumination may emerge from the void, wrote: "Truly, it is in the darkness that one finds the light, so when we are in sorrow, there this light is nearest of all to us."

5. Emergence

Emergence is identified with the psychological state called "verification," where one tests the functionality of the new solution in one's life. Renewed and revitalized, you emerge from the dark night of the soul eager to participate in all of your life from a new and enhanced perspective. With supreme faith, you joyfully reap the results of your inner work. Sometimes the results manifest externally at the very moment of emergence; sometimes they are left to ripen on the vine for some future flowering beyond your current, imaginings. Regardless of what fate brings to you, in emergence you have a sense of the universe working *through* you toward some greater purpose, often in ways beyond your understanding or your control. On a profound level, you accept fully that given who you are, where you've come from, and the circumstances you face, you are in exactly the right place and time doing precisely the right things to the best of your ability. You experience yourself as being aligned with unseen forces working through you.

This does not mean you have the capability of getting everything to turn out the way you want each and every time. You will make mistakes. You will fail. But when you emerge from the dark night, you will find yourself able to accept the failures and disappointments life inevitably brings your way, feeling your emotions fully, and moving on with or without them. You will trust that however convoluted your journey may appear to yourself and to others, you are always fulfilling your destiny the fastest, most direct way possible for you. It is only your limited human perceptions that prevent you from seeing the grand scheme. In truth, there are no dead ends. There are only adventures along the way. Life is a process, not a goal.

This is a life based on faith. To justify living in this way may not be provable—but it can be the most logical option. As Joseph F. Byrnes defines faith, in his book *The Psychology of Religion: "Faith is a sensible cognitive operation resting on probabilities."*

When you see your life in this way, you no longer need to put your vital energy into protecting yourself from pain. You surrender to the experiences circumstances bring to you, embracing rather than resisting your problems. When you can do this, your full potential will be available to you—the potential to live, serve, and create.

In *Leaves of Grass,* Walt Whitman describes the experience of emergence:

O to confront night, storms, hunger, ridicule,
accidents, rebuffs, as the trees and animals do
Dear Camerado! I confess I have urged you onward
with me, and still urge you, without the least
idea of what is our destination,
Or whether we shall be victorious, or utterly
quell'd and defeated

✳

These are the five stages one encounters while traversing the void. As you have seen, they correspond to similar stages proposed by psychology researchers. But despite their scientific support, they are not linear. They are not rational. They are not even particularly conscious. There is really nothing you can do to make this process happen for you. In fact, the only thing you can do is to set your intention and become willing to engage with whatever arises. It takes courage to be this open to one's authentic experience, the ability to pierce one's illusions of control and comfort in order to gain access to the deeper material of one's consciousness.

If you did everything within your current level of ability to experience your emotions fully, and yet did not have any particular breakthrough in this last hour, you may be tempted to believe that the problem is that you didn't experience your emotions authentically enough. Authentically enough compared to what? This is the kind of dualistic thinking Eastern philosophy strives to overcome by transcending the emotions—and that we Westerners strive to overcome by exhausting them.

You can experience emergence the moment you give up judging your experiences. So many of us have bought the notion that it is our positive thinking that will bring us the experience we want. But what happens when you become depressed? Are you doomed? The truth is, you can have a positive attitude and still be disappointed in life; and you can be depressed and have something great happen to you five minutes from now. Either situation brings you face to face with the truth of the matter: that you are not in control of your destiny.

You can influence your fate—and certainly you should do what you can to get things to turn out well for you. But that's all you can do. When things are going great for you, it's easy to forget this. The gift of the leaner times in your life is that you are given the precious opportunity to peek through the illusions that normally block your view—and into the mystery beyond. Remember, it is neither your happy emotions nor your fearful ones that create your reality. There are forces at work in your life far greater than your moods and emotions. Do what you can to influence positively the circumstances that fate hands you by doing everything within your power to the best of your ability, and then let it go. This you can do sad or happy, anxious or optimistic.

Take it on faith that you can use everything that life sends your way—the things you want, the things you don't. When you stop pushing, driving, and striving for things to be different, you bring yourself into alignment with unseen powers. Your process becomes the process of the divine working through you.

Just as David could not trust his emotions to tell him the truth about reality when he was giving his speech to the defense industry executives, you cannot trust your emotions that urge you to judge yourself as a failure in the process I just asked you to do—or in your life.

Spirit works invisibly. It is like a river, flowing freely until it hits an obstacle. Then, it pauses—pooling up upon itself—until it rises high enough to push over to the other side. *The I Ching* notes what you have observed for yourself: "If increase goes on unceasingly, there is bound to be a breakthrough." Remember, when you try to look at the dammed water from the other side of the wall, you cannot see it rise until that one last drop carries it over the top.

Similarly, inner work, done with good intention, is never wasted. Every drop contributes to raising your level. It is a totally efficient process. Perhaps you are not yet ready to say "Ah, so" to your problems and experiences, but certainly you will be willing to suspend your judgment until sunset tonight to give your hardworking mind just one day in which to practice solving your problems in the new way I am teaching to you.

You can't trust your emotions to provide you with an accurate reflection of reality—but your emotions are good for something. They are the way into the inner workings of your cognitive structures. The way to progress is to be fully where you are right now, regardless of the results you have or haven't gotten, and then, simply to do what's next.

HOUR
NUMBER
THREE

Telling the Story of Your Life

Six

Paradise Lost

By now, your problem has been solved; you haven't resolved it yet, but you trust the *Solved by Sunset* process; or you are feeling somewhere between let down and downright upset. To those of you in the third camp, one more thought about feelings before we move on to the next exercise. By now you know that I do not believe that emotions equate to reality. But this does not mean you don't have to deal with them in the real world of your everyday life, right here, right now. In fact, your emotions will be very helpful to you in this next process—and in the processes to come. The trick is to learn to have your emotions—not to let your emotions have you.

What do I mean by this? One useful way of getting a grip on feelings is to approach them in the same way you think about the weather. You know you can't make the sun shine or the wind die down. If you hate bad weather, you protect yourself from it as best you can by snuggling up by the fire. If you must go out, you grab your scarf or your umbrella and boots and dash about spending as little time in it as you can, possibly grumbling as you go.

Perhaps you love a good storm, and you put on your galoshes to rush out for a hike in the woods. Neither of these responses is any more valid than the other. Your attitude and reaction are completely up to you. Chances are you will not be judged by others, or by yourself, whatever your response. Because the weather is something you recognize as beyond your control, you see it as something outside of you that will pass.

So it can be with your emotions. Bracketing your descent does not mean you won't have feelings anymore. But it can mean that you won't have to be at their beck and call. You may not always be in a position to control your emotions—but you can learn how to move forward with them. A storm of upset can be moving in from the west at 20 knots. You can put a kettle of tea on the fire and wait patiently for it to pass; you can grab your umbrella and rush about grumbling against it; or you can put on your boots and splash around in it. It will pass. Tomorrow will be partly bittersweet with a chance of fulfillment. It is the nature of the universe that sooner or later weather more to your liking is bound to arrive.

The I Ching teaches us that everything is in constant motion, strengthening or weakening on a continual basis. Night turns into day, drought gives way to flood. When any particular aspect peaks, it spontaneously turns into its opposite. *The I Ching* takes this concept from nature. Pointing to the cycles of the seasons, the ancient Chinese recognized that each quality contains its antithesis: at the depth of winter, roots of spring are preparing to bloom. In the autumn, yesterday's leaves return to the earth to fertilize new ground. So it is that at the peak of sadness, one may suddenly burst open with the laughter of fresh perspective. Or at the height of joy, one feels an inexplicable sadness. The moments when any affect turns into its opposite is a "turning point." These are moments of opportunity. If your emotions are at the surface right now, consider yourself blessed.

The wise individual learns to use these peak moments to gain access into the inner workings of his or her cognitive processes.

Not that this is an easy lesson to learn. Not quite two years ago, just before our move to Nashville, Dan and I hosted a good-bye party for some of our closest San Francisco friends. We received many uplifting farewell gifts: heart-shaped picture frames with special photographs, care packages of Peet's Coffee and sourdough starter, and so on. I didn't expect that anyone would give me a present that would upset me. But toward the end of the party, one of my wisest, dearest friends gave me a carved, wooden figure taken from the ancient Chinese spiritual tradition. The figure's head was bent down sorrowfully into his arms. I would have understood if my friend had told me this was how she was feeling about my moving away. But instead the sentiment that accompanied the gift was her hope that this figure would bring me luck in Nashville. At the time, I felt that the little wooden figure was an omen of unhappiness. It was her subtle, and not very encouraging way, of letting me know that when my little adventure failed, she'd be there to pick up the pieces. I hid the little figure in the bottom of one of the many boxes that we sent on ahead of us to our new home, the box titled "Knickknacks— open last."

Several weeks later, having exhausted the adrenaline of the move by unpacking crates of pans, lamps, and office equipment, I finally caught a moment to breathe. The heart-shaped photo frame was on the piano, Peet's coffee was perking in the new kitchen.

Rather than the relief I'd expected to encounter, I found myself feeling the great loss of what I had left behind—and the mountain of new experiences I had yet to climb. What had seemed exciting —if terrifying—now seemed simply terrifying. The heart-shaped picture, as much as it had cheered me to that very moment, now seemed woefully inadequate—a child's thumb to help hold the water of grief behind the dike.

Thankfully, I remembered that there was one box left to unpack:

the box of knickknacks. Tearing through plastic bubble wrap, I found my treasure: the little wooden figure. Somebody, thousands of years ago, and someone else, several weeks ago, had understood what I would be going through today. This was sad Buddha—the bluer notes of the range of the universe's greatest gift: the full spectrum of what it means to be fully alive. This little figure gave me permission to go into rather than avoid my sadness—to see God's hand even in these darkest notes of the emotional scale. Ironically, it was the gift that had so upset me before I'd left San Francisco that now offered me the greatest comfort in my strange new home.

This sadness you feel, too, is as old as time. Of course you would like to solve your problem—and to feel happy and fulfilled once again. This will come. But understand first that there is a reason why this particular problem has come up for you to resolve at this point. It is not an obstacle to your happiness, but the very vehicle of your deliverance to a new stage of growth. As long as you are alive and growing, you will have problems. You will outgrow your ability to contain and control your past level of challenges to engage in your next stage of evolution. This does not mean you will condemn yourself to a future of emotional upheaval, however. For while it is not possible to gain mastery over fate, it is possible to gain mastery over your emotions. You do this when you learn to let your feelings roll in and through your life without getting yourself hooked into self-hatred or self-pity. One way to disengage from emotional upheaval is to become willing to tell the whole truth. You will always have problems, but at least by telling the truth you can assure yourself of having higher-quality problems.

One place to begin is by acknowledging that today's problem has come up for you before. In fact, it has presented itself to you over and over again in different forms, at different times and in different places. It is part of the story of your life: Its history is deeply rooted in your personal mythology. What do I mean by mythology? Sam Keen and Anne Valley Fox in *Telling Your Story* explain:

So long as human beings change and make history, so long as children are born and old people die, there will be tales to explain why sorrow darkens the day and stars fill the night. We invent stories about the origin and conclusion of life because . . . they help us find our way, our place at the heart of the mystery.

From the beginning of time, people have told the story of their lives in the form of fairy tales and myths. These stories not only help us gain perspective over where we've come from, but contain powerful messages that point us in the direction of where we're going. As the philosopher Rollo May explains, "Myths are like the beams in a house: not exposed to outside view, they are the structure which holds the house together so people can live in it." You were born into your own original myth: a story starring you as the hero.

In the beginning, you were whole and happy. You may have to go very far back to find this moment in your story—perhaps even before your birth. But there was a time when you were in paradise. Then something happened. Whatever it was, it took you from unity with the divine and thrust you into your life adventure. Suddenly, there were challenges to be overcome. Problems to be solved. The quest you chose to undertake and the way you chose to resolve your issues form the crux of your personal mythology.

Perhaps you have a dynamic mythology—like the knights of King Arthur's Court whom I wrote of earlier, who allowed their curiosity concerning the nature of the unveiled Holy Grail to inspire their adventure. Their response was to leave behind the status quo of everyday life, willingly striking out alone into the darkest night in order to fulfill their quest. This is a mission that could last a lifetime —a quest worthy of them.

But it is also possible that your original myth, while working well for you at the time, did not have the breadth and depth of vision necessary to inspire an entire lifetime. For instance, you may have adopted a variation of the heroic theme, but one with very different ramifications: the archetype of the Steadfast Tin Soldier. In this story, the hero, hopelessly in love with a paper ballerina in another part of the toy room, squashes first the expression of his love, and then his cry for help, in order to preserve his air of propriety. After one brave attempt to cross the abyss that sadly misfires, he becomes a victim of circumstances ending up melting into a puddle of lead and the ballerina's subsequent flaming to ash.

Although the Holy Grail may also be pursued in this manner, the Tin Soldier is not acting out of passionate vitality, but rather against rejection and loneliness. He may look and act bravely, but a destructive pattern is building. He is going through the motions of heroism, but feeling all the while a victim. This is a personal mythology that may work well short term, but will not endure the span of a lifetime.

This is but one of many myths. For every Steadfast Tin Soldier, there is a Poor Little Match Girl. There are Samsons and Little Mermaids. There are even Elvis Presleys and Princess Dianas. The books of Joseph Campbell, Carl Jung, and Clarissa Pinkola Estes can help you place your personal myth in archetypal and historical context. But regardless of whether or not you take the time to find your prototype in literature, you can participate in a process that will help you identify the particular story you've adopted and that has contributed to the problem you are facing today. Understand that this is not an occasion for guilt or remorse. Your myth may have been passed to you through your family system, or even through your genes. However, it came to you; it served you at the time or you would not have kept it with you for so long. But know this: that for every problem your myth solved, there was a price to be paid. This is the note that has come due for payment in the form of today's problem.

By getting to know your original myth, you will come to better understand the meaning and purpose of your present problem. You will see your issue in the context of your life history. This requires courage, because you will need to tell the truth about old, old patterns that have been working for you well enough for quite some time, and you will have to enter new terrain, with all the attendent risks, in order to create a new, healthier myth.

As we discussed the concept of cycles earlier in this chapter, so do we now revisit the idea in relation to your personal mythology. The forces of nature are constantly creating and destroying in order to clear the way for new growth. When you are fully alive, you are continually letting go of what you have, making space for new possibilities to come to you. You channel your vital energy into finding greater opportunities for your growth, rather than using your essential spirit to protect what you currently have. Your life can be an expanding spiral—rather than a closed-end circle—each turn growing wider and wider. Where are you in this life spiral right now? Are you near the bottom with a narrow focus, going around and around over the same ground, your problem seeming large and insolvable? Or are you allowing yourself to move up the spiral, letting go of the past so that you can relax into an expanded vision of your potential? It is around the very next turn of the spiral that the solution to your problem will spontaneously occur to you.

We are ready now for the third hour's process: the reassessment of your original mythology and the generation of a new personal myth—one that is worthy of you.

❋ Process: *Putting Your Problem in Context*

This is another writing exercise. As in the example drawn from *The I Ching* of the pot of water boiling over an open fire, you will be seeking to find that place of balance between thinking and intuition where the forces are in correct relationship and the boiling water can do its work.

To assist you in establishing this balance, I will ask you a series of questions that will cause you to call upon both your rational cognitive functions—memory and analysis, for instance—and the more intuitive processes that we've been utilizing exclusively to this point.

What I am asking you to do in this hour's assignment is to find the threads of meaning underlying your original myth—and see if you can find the roots of your current problem in the solutions of your own past. Out of this, you will have the opportunity to create a new personal myth for yourself—one that holds the potential to resolve the issue you are facing today and reinvigorates the very nature of your life's adventure by bringing you into alignment with the hidden order of the universe.

Because this is a challenging assignment, you may be tempted to ask yourself at this point whether the problem you have selected to work with today is really the best one for you. You may doubt your answers, your choices, and your creative, intuitive responses. I'm here to suggest that you can relax about this.

Researchers David Feinstein and Stanley Krupps in their work on the subject of personal mythology teach us about the phenomenon they called the "holographic principle":

> Each part of a hologram contains information from every other part. In a similar manner, whatever personal myth you may be examining in some fundamental way embodies your entire mythic system. Working through one area may have repercussions on many areas. Therefore, it is far less important that you select what you rationally deduce to be the "ideal" conflict than that you select an area for which you have some feeling.

The holographic principle gives you permission to stop worrying about doing this right. All you need to do is to take each of these questions in order. Avoid the temptation to look ahead. Instead, consider them one by one, giving yourself several minutes to tap into the truest answer that occurs to you before you write it down. If nothing occurs to you, make something up. Write down whatever pops into your mind. If you don't already have your paper and pen with you, go and get it now and then we will begin.

✳ Now, write your answers to the following questions:

1. What is your earliest happy memory? Think of a time when you felt whole, connected, happy, fulfilled. Fill the memory in with as much detail as possible. Where were you? What were you wearing? Who was with you? What happened? How did you feel?

2. What interrupted that happiness? What came up for you that got in the way of the experience of being whole, happy, fully alive? Where were you? What clothes were you wearing? What shoes did you have on your feet? Who was with you? What happened? Again, fill in the memory with as much detail as you can. Do not worry about accuracy here, but rather about capturing the event or situation with all of the feelings that come with it.

3. What was your solution? How did you handle the interruption? What did you do? See yourself at a moment in which the solution crystallized and you knew what you had to do to survive. What changes did you make? How did you begin to act? What life decisions did you make as a result of the interruption? What beliefs did you adopt?

4. What good came of your solution? How did your solution work for you? How did your solution reduce the pain? How did it help you survive? How did it protect you? Envision yourself at a time when the solution was being effective for you. Who is with you? What are you wearing? Where are you? What else do you remember about this incident?

5. What price did you have to pay for this solution? What harm came of it? What did you have to sacrifice? What new problems came up for you as a result of your solution? Recall an incident where your solution cost you something. What did you give up? How did it feel?

6. How is the thing that you sacrificed so long ago still affecting you? How does it relate to the problem you want to resolve today?

Put your pen down for a few moments and take several deep breaths. If you are not already feeling the emotions connected to these questions, this is a good opportunity to deepen the process. Bracket your emotions once again, and give yourself permission to really experience the feelings attached to these six questions for the remainder of this exercise. In a minute, I'm going to ask you to get back fully into right-brain consciousness and let your imagination run free. Don't direct this next part of the process in order to make your writing come out any certain way. Rather, respond to my directions by allowing images to arise spontaneously in your consciousness. The more fanciful, wild, weird, or irrational your thoughts are, the better. Let yourself have fun with this assignment —even if the "fun" is accompanied by sighs and tears. Nothing is out of bounds: your story can include dragons, flying saucers, characters from fiction, anything and everything that occurs to you.

Are you ready?

Good. I want you to tell me the myth that has been operating in your life.

✸ Process: *Your Personal Myth*

Begin with the words:

1. "Once upon a time, there was a happy child named . . ."
When you have pictured this child's idyllic situation in as much detail as possible, continue the story with these words.

2. "Then something terrible happened."
When you have detailed the terrible thing that happened, continue with these words.

3. "The brave little child knew what had to be done."
Tell the story of how the little child solved the problem. What adventures did the child have as a result? What struggles did the child face? What quest did the child take on as a result of the terrible thing that happened? What was the outcome of the child's adventures? After detailing this part of the story, it will be time to come to a conclusion. Do so with the following words:

4. "And they all lived happily ever after."
Take a moment to celebrate. If you can't celebrate the artistry of your story, at least celebrate the effort you put into it. We are about to move on, but before we do, this is important: What lesson does this myth illustrate? Did the ending fit the rest of the story? Was there dissonance in the words *happily ever after*? Did it ring true or false? And finally, take a moment to think about the point of it all— the underlying theme and teaching. Then write the last section of your myth:

5. "The moral of this story is . . ."
Go ahead. Before you read on, take the time to capture the moral of the story in one or at most two well-thought-out sentences.

Now let me ask you something. This may be a moral that worked for you back then, once upon a time, but does it work for you now? Or have you outgrown your original myth and now need to create a new storyline for your life? You will know that this is a myth that is current, vital, and alive by asking yourself one more question:

Does the moral of the myth you just wrote down resolve your current problem?

If it does, congratulations! You have solved your problem by sunset. All you needed to do was tap into the wisdom of your life story and apply it to your current situation.

If it does not, congratulations are due you as well! You have evolved to a new level of awareness. And this new level of spiritual growth merits a new personal myth. You now have the opportunity to develop a new myth for yourself. What a relief it is to realize that there is nothing about your history that dictates who you must be today—how you have to relate and react to the challenges you face. Regardless of the external circumstances you face in your life, your inner world is yours alone—a place where, if you have the courage to take on the responsibility of it, you can be free.

Take the time to try it for yourself: Revisit your myth and rewrite it just the way you would like it to be now. You can use the same beginning and development you used in the myth exercise above (numbers 1 and 2). But then try spinning your story off in a new direction. Keep trying out new possibilities for numbers 3 through 5 until your hero gets the result he or she truly deserves: one that will work for you now. This will be a better way of responding to life's challenges than the old myth that worked for you in the past.

Seven

✦

Honoring Your Story

We do not see things as they are. We see them as we are.
—Talmud

Your mythology is a reflection of who you are at this moment, and it can help you understand how the problem you are dealing with today fits into the overall context of your life. If you are unhappy with the results of your creative effort, remember that as long as you are alive, you are still in the middle of your story. If you don't like your myth—you can rewrite it at any time.

I remember the first time I did this process with a workshop group. One of my friends, Stacy, had volunteered to be one of my guinea pigs. I knew her to be a great mother—but someone who often became overly involved with both the successes and disappointments of her two daughters. When one got the lead part in a community production, Stacy was over the moon. When the invitation to a much-anticipated birthday party failed to materialize for one of her girls, she felt she had somehow failed. It was at such a moment of despair that she had been asked to write the myth of her life. I asked her not to worry about the literal accuracy of her story. Instead, I suggested that she feel her way through the plot, letting her emotions and intuition lead the way. Here is the result:

> Once upon a time, there was a young princess named Savannah who was the best beloved of her father and mother, the king and queen. Then something terrible happened. A horrible war broke out with a neighboring kingdom and she was kidnapped by the enemy, an evil knight named Marduk. The evil knight took Savannah far away to his land, locking the princess in his castle, expecting to use her as ransom. Not knowing this, she assumed that she was going to be there forever. It was unbearable to think of this possibility. Savannah wanted to kick and scream and shout; but that, she decided, would be far too dangerous. Instead she sought a means of escape, but she could find no way out.
>
> Suddenly, the brave little girl knew what had to be done. She decided that she would do everything he asked of her— better than he expected. In this way, perhaps he would come to love her enough to let her go. When his dishes were dirty, Savannah washed them. When he was sad, she danced for him. Meanwhile, unbeknownst to Savannah, the evil knight was negotiating with her parents for her return. The money for her release arrived. But by then, Marduk was so entranced by the princess that he no longer wanted to release her. In fact, no amount of money would have induced him to let Savannah go. The princess, ignorant of her parents' efforts to retrieve her, continued to live with the evil knight, eventually coming to care for him as much as he cared for her. And they lived happily ever after.
>
> The moral of the story is: When problems come your way, squash your real feelings in order to survive, and while you might not get what you really want out of life, you may learn to appreciate what it is you do end up with.

This is the story Stacy told, but she really didn't like it very much. And when she tried to apply the moral to her current issue, her perceived failure as a parent, she ended up feeling worse. I asked her if she'd like to take a crack at rewriting her myth. She grabbed at the chance. As she told her fellow guinea pigs later, she began following her feelings of sadness for the princess who had so bravely done what she thought she had to do. It was so apparent to her what Savannah's compliance had cost her. The princess had become trapped by the very vehicle that she had mistakenly thought would be her means of escape: her ability to please others. Had she followed her innate urge to be feisty and unpleasant, she would have been spit out of the abusive system and returned to her natural home. As this thought occurred to Stacy, she grabbed her pen to rewrite the myth.

This time the little princess knew just what to do. She would tell Marduk at every opportunity how much she wanted to go home and how mean he was. If Savannah were annoying enough, he would let her go that much sooner. Sure enough, the ransom arrived and he was thrilled to let her go. And Savannah lived much more happily ever after.

The moral of the new myth Stacy came up with was this: *It is better to be your real self and have problems than to squash your real self in order to solve your problems.*

When she applied this moral to her parenting issues, she had the resolution she sought. For starters, she realized that she had been unknowingly feeling that if her children were more pleasing to others, they wouldn't be having problems (the invitation would have arrived as hoped for). But taking the lesson from her story, Stacy realized that she would rather they be their real selves and not be invited than sacrifice their authenticity in order to be popular.

Rather than feeling bad about this "failure," she began to feel good about her children's abilities to be true to themselves. Rather than be upset with her parenting, she felt proud. The situation had literally turned upside down. The issue she had hoped to resolve by sunset magically lifted. This would have been enough—but there was more.

In considering the original myth she had created, Stacy saw how much of her vital energy had been invested in trying to please others in order to be loved. She had sacrificed her authentic expression of who she really was in exchange for comfort. In equating love with protection, she had unwittingly adopted the subconscious belief that her children could only love her to the degree to which she could protect them from the pain of life's bumps and bruises. She had taken pride in her parenting when she succeeded and felt herself to be a failure when she fell short.

To give up the feelings of pride and failure that were the hallmarks of her parenting experience over the years would be to admit to the limits of her power and control in relation to her daughter's experiences. Could such a "useless" human being nevertheless find a place for herself as part of God's creation? To shift to the new myth would require Stacy to take a risk of this magnitude. What if she gave up her desire to please and protect, and nothing came to take its place? What if she were truly authentic—but as a result, nobody wanted to stick around? *Was the ransom really on its way?*

The relinquishment of one's old mythology is never to be taken lightly. The questions Stacy asked herself at this juncture may seem superficial or even pathetic to the outside observer. But from where Stacy stood, they seemed no less than a question of life or death. And, in point of fact, it was: the life or death of her very spirit was at stake.

The personal myth that had served her so well for so many decades of her life now seemed woefully inadequate. Had she not been guided to rewrite her myth, she may well have assumed that her hope for future happiness depended on getting her child on that invitation list. (Indeed, I have witnessed more than one individual getting stuck in the mire for months, years, decades, or even a lifetime on issues not much more substantial than getting on the right invitation list: admission to the right medical school, for instance, or making the swim team.) Instead, Stacy realized she had become overly invested in her daughters' lives at the expense of her own vitality. It was not her job to make everything turn out for her children. Her job was to love her kids, no matter how things were turning out for them. Making the transition to living her own life— and staying on her own side of the line in relation to theirs—would be worth the risk. It would take great discipline, but it would provide great payoffs.

It takes tremendous faith and a degree of spiritual giftedness to release your old myth. To move on, you must first be willing to grieve for what no longer works for you, letting yourself feel the pain for what your original solutions have cost you, and realizing why you needed to go to these extremes in the first place. But there's something you must do that will require even more courage. You must be able to forgive yourself for your original myth. And then you must go even further. You must be willing to honor yourself for having created it—and for being willing to question it as well. Our lives move through stages. We must find the good not only in what we are becoming—but also in what we have been.

In her book *Gift from the Sea,* Anne Morrow Lindbergh wrote:

> How can one learn to live through the ebb tides of one's existence? How can one learn to take the trough of the wave? It is easier to understand here on the beach, where the breathlessly still ebb-tides reveal another life below the level which mortals usually reach. In this crystalling moment of suspense, one has a sudden revelation of the secret kingdom at the bottom of the sea. . . . Perhaps this is the most important thing for me to take back from beach-living: simply the memory that each cycle of the tide is valid; each cycle of the wave is valid; each cycle of a relationship is valid. And my shells? I can sweep them all into my pocket. They are only there to remind me that the sea recedes and returns eternally.

Thunderstruck

Eight

Unseen Forces

When your personal myth is outdated, the pipeline that connects you to your natural intuition is clogged with beliefs that no longer work for you, and with the fear and anxiety that are their unwelcome by-products. The first hours of this day have been dedicated to clearing away some of the obstructions—enough, at any rate, to let some light and air through. As you have seen through my examples—and I hope through your own growing bank of personal evidence—when you overwhelm your left-brain "you-can-make-it happen" approaches to problem-solving with receiving-letting-being right-brain experiences, you can suddenly find yourself with expanded clarity and insight. Whether or not your problem has already been resolved to your satisfaction, it is likely that at the very least you will find yourself more willing and more able to trade the illusion of your control over the things that happen to you for a newfound grasp on reality. The more you become willing to see things as they are, the more likely you are to make better decisions. Why? Because you will be more in touch with what is true. You might not like what the facts are, but at least you will know that what you are dealing with is real. If all that happens as a result of the *Solved by Sunset* process is that your vision clarifies and your perception expands, it will be enough. You will manage your issues and your life more effectively. You will find yourself with an increased ability to resolve your problems quickly and with insight. But I believe there's more. You may recall that the *Solved by Sunset* process is based on three assumptions. Now I am ready to let you in on a secret. There is a fourth. Before I tell you what this fourth assumption is, let's take a moment to review the first three.

Assumption Number One: There is an unseen order in the universe.

Assumption Number Two: Your highest good lies in harmoniously adjusting yourself to this unseen order.

Assumption Number Three: Whatever keeps you from experiencing your alignment with the universe is accidental, and can be overcome.

These first three assumptions act as a bridge from your active, rational processes to your intuitive, receptive experiences. But as spiritual as they are, they nevertheless place the responsibility on *your* shoulders of becoming aligned with the unseen order. It appears to be *your* task to adjust harmoniously to the universe's life force. It is *your* challenge to overcome the obstacles that separate you from alignment. It is even *your* challenge to be willing to take on the struggle to live fully.

These three assumptions are foundational, but without a fourth, they would be incomplete, even misleading. For it is not only up to you to do what it takes to solve your problems. When you become willing to engage sincerely in the task of being fully alive, you create an increased opportunity for forces beyond your comprehension to engage in your problem-solving process.

Intuition, you may recall, is defined as "a spiritual influence that occurs spontaneously and renders a person capable of thinking, speaking, or acting in ways that transcend ordinary capacities." We have been talking often of these unseen forces. You have been clearing the channels that have the capability of consciously connecting you to these forces: doing the inner work, preparing yourself for alignment with them. Now, at last, it is time to release your personal will and responsibility. Once you do this, you will be allowing for the possibility of spontaneous interaction with unseen forces.

William James describes this as a state of mind "in which the will to assert ourselves and hold our own has been displaced by a willingness to close our mouths and be as nothing in the floods and waterspouts of God."

Therefore, I propose we take the following as our fourth assumption:

Assumption Number Four: Forces beyond your comprehension are already engaged in your problem-solving process.

You do not need to be in any particular frame of mind to become suddenly conscious of these unseen forces. In fact, you may well be upset, depressed, or anxious—and still you can be overtaken. In order to bring the interaction to a conscious level, one's own rational processes must be at least temporarily replaced by a spontaneous receptivity to extraordinary experience. In truth, this displacement of will may actually be part of the process, occur simultaneously with it, or even be a primary function of the unseen powers. Rather than the more linear cause-and-effect model, in which transcendence of left-brain thinking is the *prerequisite,* such an experience of transformation *always* finds its roots in the unseen powers, rather than in you. Therefore you need not be in any particular state of mind or spirit in order to have it happen. It asks nothing of you other than that you be overwhelmed by it. In 1854, Henry David Thoreau wrote an account of such a revelation that took place during his time of solitude at Walden Pond:

Once, a few weeks after I came to the woods, for an hour I doubted whether the near neighborhood of man was not essential to the serene and healthy life. To be alone was somewhat unpleasant. But, in the midst of a gentle rain, while these thoughts prevailed, I was suddenly sensible of such sweet and beneficient society in nature, in the very pattering of the drops, and in every sight and sound around my house, an infinite and unaccountable friendliness all at once, like an atmosphere, sustaining me. . . . Every little pine needle expanded and swelled with sympathy of something kindred to me, that I thought no place could ever be strange to me again.

The transformative experience can take many forms—from Thoreau's quiet homecoming to Archimedes' ebullient "Eureka!"; from a South American shaman's trance to the biblical prophets' ecstatic swoon. (When first encountering the divine, the prophet Ezekial sat "estonied" with the enormity of it all for seven days.) Despite the variety of modes of its expression, all who have come into contact with these unseen powers have had one experience in common: they are clear that something extraordinary has transpired that has somehow changed them for the better.

In my own case, my first conscious recognition that I was engaging with a power greater than myself came under the most extreme of circumstances. It was a situation so terrifying that I am only able to write about it fully now, seventeen years after it took place. It was a pivotal event in my life because in its midst, I was forced to change paradigms—or die.

This turning point in my life came at the age of thirty. Married for ten years, too busy and involved in our life together to have children, Dan and I teetered precariously on the threshhold between youth and adulthood. We were each full of dreams and vital energy, but we had reached a moment of decision. The public relations agency I had founded in San Francisco was just starting to blossom, but Dan's desire to pursue a career in music was calling for us to move to either Los Angeles or Nashville, both centers of the industry. Neither of us was willing to give up any ground for the other—not because we didn't love each other, but because we each felt our creative potential was, at that moment, the stronger of the urges and we were afraid to deny our spirits' calls.

During this period, Dan made the decision to travel to music industry centers to look into opportunities, while I stayed behind in San Francisco. I knew we were at some kind of crossroads, but I could not read the signals as to which of the options that presented themselves to us represented growth and which were regression. Should I move with Dan? Should Dan stay in San Francisco? Should we stay together? Should we separate? Rather than do the wrong thing, I did nothing. I hoped, I suppose, that somehow the pain would all go away and we would resume life as usual. Meanwhile, Dan had packed his antique Studebaker and hit the road. And so it was, that on a rare, hot summer night in San Francisco, I turned off the lights in the upstairs bedroom of our Victorian house on California Street and tried to sleep.

Sometime in the middle of the night, a burglar found an open window in the downstairs living room which was exactly the invitation he had been looking for. Closing the windows and locking the doors at night had been Dan's job. Meanwhile I lived in the receding fantasies of childhood that held that nothing bad would ever happen to someone like me. My marriage would be just fine, the weather would be pleasantly balmy on a full moon night, and doors and windows did not need to be checked before I went to bed.

Then suddenly, there was a leather-gloved hand at my throat choking back the scream that I was too frightened to make. And in the other hand was a straight-edged razor. His face was masked and his body clothed in black leather. He was death in my bedroom and at my throat.

"Get me your money!" he growled at me, pushing me toward the bedroom dresser. I did not have money to give him. Dan was the one who dealt with money stuff. At that desperate moment, I wasn't even sure where my purse was. When I hesitated, I felt the razor graze my chest, staining my nightgown red, and then time suddenly stopped. It was as if the next few moments, while taking less than a minute in real time, stretched for an eternity. Reality cracked open and I could distinctly hear a voice issuing from my soul:

Live or die? The choice is yours. You can take the easy way out now and it will all be over before you know it. Or you can turn your life over to me and start over again. It will be hard, it will be painful—but it will be worth it. It's up to you. Choose. Choose now.

I knew that the voice was the voice of life itself, making me an offer that went beyond the current crisis—it went to the very roots of how I had been choosing to live. Until that moment, I had believed that I was specially selected to succeed. Life was about comfort and getting my way. Dan's conflicting desires upset my notions about how my life was meant to be. God had put me at an unfair advantage by denying me what I wanted. And now I was being shown the results of how I had been approaching my life.

You want the easy way? Where doors don't need to be locked and love makes no unfair demands on you? Here's the solution—your means of deliverance to an existence without pain: a straight-edged razor at your throat.

The situation was impossible. There was no way out. And yet, suddenly, I knew without a doubt that the answer to the question I suddenly faced was simple and clear:

YES! I want to live. I take all the encumbrances, responsibilities, pain, and limitation that this entails. I take it all. I see now, it's worth it—worth every bit of it. Just help me live through this and I will be Yours to use as Your instrument on this earth for as long as I live.

From that moment on, my body and voice acted instinctively—there was no mind in it. I said words I couldn't possibly have thought, came up with things I did not know I knew, and acted in ways I did not think possible. In short, I got the burglar to walk with me, blade to my throat, down the long stairway to the first floor where, I said, we kept our cash. Instead, I walked him to a drawer I had never had occasion to open before. Dan had, when we first moved into the Victorian house some years ago, and unbeknownst to me, placed a big pair of scissors there. I grabbed them and wheeled around to stab the burglar in the chest. The scissors did not deeply penetrate his layers of dark clothing, but the action startled him enough that he released his grip and bolted for the front door and out into the darkness.

Since that night I have never doubted that there are unseen powers at work in my life. Many things changed for me as a result of this experience. Changed for both Dan and myself; he was as shaken by his near-loss as I was. We realized that our love was as important to us as our dreams—and well worth sacrificing for. We each confronted the fact that life's choices were more complex than our youthful illusions had led us to believe. I began locking doors, participating in our banking responsibilities, and studying martial arts. Dan and I began to work together as a true team, engaging in the dance of life first as a couple, then, nine months later, as a growing family. We learned about compromising in the name of love, deferring gratification, tending our own and each other's dreams, railing together when fate is unfair, celebrating when it is sweet. The ramifications of that night still continue to unfold as we celebrate the sixteenth birthday of our son, the tenth of our daughter, and the recent appointment of the Nashville-based image development company Dan Orsborn Public Relations as an agency to Warner Brothers Records. Dan is in the music industry at last.

The experience of divine communication can be yours also—you need only to become receptive to it. For some people who are, perhaps, more spiritually gifted than I, it may come as a "still, small voice." In my case, a sledgehammer seems to have been required. I did not choose to be receptive. I simply, dramatically, and rather quickly exhausted all my other options. Only then did the voice call to me.

In the next chapter of *Solved by Sunset,* you will be introduced to four different means by which you may become increasingly receptive to receiving wisdom, knowledge, information, and direction from a source other than that which you access through everyday consciousness. If you prefer to think of this expanded awareness as coming from your own unconscious, it will work for you just as well. At this point, the important thing is not that you believe in the unseen powers of the universe, but that you are, as the Twelve-Step programs teach us, willing to act *as if* such extraordinary revelation is possible—however it expresses itself to you. In the spiritual realm and in many traditions, not knowing is considered a higher state than certainty, for at the very least, you have given up the arrogant illusion of control. Realizing that we are *not* in control is, in fact, the essence of faith. For if you did know exactly what was going to happen to you, why would you need faith? Faith invites us to set aside our rational processes to engage with the mystery.

Nine

✴

The Choice Is Yours

In a moment, you will be given instructions for Thunderstruck, the exercise that will highlight your fourth hour. This is a powerful process—one that holds the possibility of rendering you capable of thinking, speaking, or acting in ways that transcend your ordinary capacities. But before you proceed, I would like to introduce you to some tools that you may choose to use during this hour. You may use one of these or all four, singly or in combination. Which tools you decide to try may depend on the resources you have available to you, the environment in which you are doing the *Solved by Sunset* process, and, of course, your own inner guidance.

I begin with a discussion of the most controversial of the four. Even if you choose not to use this means of developing receptivity —or if you don't have the appropriate resources at hand—please read this discussion all the way through since principles will be introduced that will be important to you, no matter which of the four tools you choose to use.

I call this first option an "intuitive decision-making tool," but you may have encountered this notion previously as "divination." At this point, you may be envisioning fortune-tellers and card readers, and neon palm-print signs. There are, of course, spiritually primitive approaches to divination that consider casting cards as magic, believing that one can use spells or rituals to foretell or influence one's fate. But that is not an approach I advocate. Instead, I am going to be teaching you a radically new approach to intuitive decision-making that happens to use divinatory tools that others have sometimes misused and misunderstood. I have taught this technique to hundreds of businesspeople, many of them skeptical or downright anxious at the prospects of pulling a card from a tarot deck. I take the risk of stepping on old fears and beliefs because so many people have been enriched by the experience, receiving guidance or support in their decision-making process along the way.

If you have a deck of tarot cards, or some other favorite form of divinatory tool on hand, you may want to use them as one of your four options. But there are two stipulations.

✸ The first is that you must promise to put aside any instruction booklets explaining the meaning of the symbology—and avoid such explanatory guides in the future. Teachers and guides who define meaning for you, who ossify the myriad possibilities into their *own* take on reality, steal your power and vitality and replace your own intuitive knowing with external direction.

(There are, by the way, a number of intuitive divinatory professionals who are sensitive, inspirational guides who can help you use cards, psychic readings, astrology, and similar divinatory tools in a constructive manner consistent with the approach I am describing. Should you retain an outside consultant in the future, the information in this chapter will provide you with a means by which to judge whether you are working with someone who is contributing to your growing freedom from the illusion of power—or taking it away.)

Rather than look for someone else's meaning when working with divinatory imagery, ask yourself what each card or symbol means to you—and do not assign permanent meaning to these, for each and every time you cast them a different, more appropriate meaning may surface. If you feel that the cards or symbols will therefore be meaningless to you, then put them aside. You are simply not resonating with them right now. You will have three other tools at your disposal.

✳ The second stipulation is that if you ever pull a card or cast a reading that feels wrong to you, one that you really don't like, throw it back and try again—or put the whole process aside and out of your thoughts.

The two forms of divination I use most frequently are *The I Ching* and the tarot. As I explained my book *How Would Confucius Ask for a Raise?*, it took me several decades to learn to use *The I Ching* because the complex imagery was poetic and verbal rather than visual. For today's purposes, therefore, and assuming that there may be newcomers to divination among my readers, I will devote my comments to the most common and classic of the divinatory tools: the Rider-Waite version of the tarot. This version lends itself particularly well to the *Solved by Sunset* process because it has visually captured seventy-eight universal, archetypal situations that can arise in both one's outer and inner lives in pictorial form. The images are complex and varied—pointing the way for you to make your own personal interpretation. I have never had a situation occur for anyone in any of my workshops that was not alluded to symbolically by one card or another. From the innocent hopes of childhood to the hero's journey into the dark night of the soul, the magician, the fool, the emperor, and the wheel of fortune. There is celebration and defeat, creativity and destruction.

When approaching an intuitive decision-making tool such as the tarot, take a moment to focus on an area of concern: What do I need to solve my problem? Is this the best course for me to take? What is getting in my way? After shuffling the cards, put them before you facedown. Then sit quietly with your question until you are fully focused. When you feel ready, pull a card from the deck. Looking at the image that presents itself, gauge your immediate and emotional responses, letting your mind wander where it will. Do not look for right and wrong answers, or predictions about your future or fate or, in fact, anything about what the card is *telling* you. Rather, look at your own reaction to it. You will find that your response may well change each time you pull any particular card. On one particular occasion, the image of a hooded man walking on a dark path with only his lantern to light the way (the Hermit) may seem terribly lonely and sad; on another occasion, the same image may seem brave and exciting. (It is a wonderful exercise in creativity to go through each card in the deck, unrelated to any particular problem or issue you are facing at the time, looking for both a possible positive and negative interpretation of each card. If you don't have a tarot deck handy, you can try this same exercise with pictures in magazines— or even with images drawn from your own dreams and fantasies.)

In psychological terms, this ability to shift perceptions is called "reframing." In both this card exercise and in the process of reframing, you train yourself to expand the possibilities for interpretation beyond the usual knee-jerk reactions. For example, you think you've been a bad parent because you've gotten angry at your child. That is a possibility. But it is also possible that your anger is a sign of how much you care about your child and that you are a terrific parent. That is reframing. You have stage fright and you think that you will never make it as a musician. Couldn't your stage fright be a reflection of your own high standards—the very drive that contains the key to your greatest potential for success?

When working with a card, picture, or dream image, write about your responses, thoughts, and emotions about the symbol or reading for five to ten minutes nonstop. It's important not to judge the writing or worry about whether it's logical or even coherent. The process you can use is very similar to the "Setting Your Intention" exercise you took part in earlier.

You can receive value from divination even if you only think of it as a tool projecting your own subconscious thoughts, and as a creative exercise generating expanded possibilities, but there is also a rich tradition in both psychological and spiritual communities that suggests that there may be something more to divination than simply letting you know what is on your mind.

Perhaps you've heard the term "synchronicity." According to Carl Jung, synchronicity takes the coincidence of events in space and time as meaning "something more" than mere chance. This "something more" represents a peculiar interdependence of objective events and the subjective state of the observer. Synchronicity is the place where science and mysticism overlap, just as our ecologically sensitive planet and diminishing resources make apparent how interrelated all things on Earth are. Use hairspray in New Jersey and the hole in the ozone layer over Antarctica is enlarged. Pollute a stream in one time zone and the cows in another produce less milk.

At the same time, the new physics have redefined the nature of reality. When we observe matter, we change its behavior. In the physical realm, it is impossible to know what ultimate truth is. Every action, no matter how minor, carries ramifications that interact infinitely with the future. The *Back to the Future* films demonstrated the transformative impact of a young girl's first kiss at a high school prom or a single bolt of lightning on events yet to come. The spiritually inspired thought "we are all one" takes on new meaning as we begin to understand that at any given moment, on some mysterious level, every action that is taking place in the universe is somehow related to every other past, simultaneous, and future action.

Jung studied synchronicity for thirty years, seeking to explain how and why the apparently random chance of tossing sticks or casting coins could result in intelligent, targeted insight beyond what accident alone could produce. When you select a card seemingly at random, it serves as a catalyst initiating your unconscious thoughts, allowing them to rise gently to the forefront of your mind. The response and insight you glean from using divination tools helps you tap in to patterns of profound meaning that are based on the notion that the card you happened to select is a reflection of your connection to the particular forces at play in the universe at that moment of time.

What synchronicity does is validate what you have most probably already intuited to be true: that there is a connection between your spiritual, emotional, and psychological states and the things that happen to you. For instance, there was the time you wanted a certain phone call to be made to you. As long as you were desperate, the phone was silent. When you finally relaxed and surrendered to the possibility that the call would not come after all, the phone suddenly started ringing. Or how about the time somebody you knew was angry, and then he was rear-ended at an intersection?

There appears to be an inherent connection in things apparently unrelated. *The I Ching* teaches us that while it is not our role to take either the credit or responsibility for creating these connections, we can study the patterns and connections that come up for us in order to better understand and respect both the laws of the universe and the inner laws of our being:

> By contemplating the forms existing in the heavens we come to understand time and its changing demands.

You do not create the whole of your reality—not in either a conscious manipulation of external reality nor by a magical manipulation of unseen powers—but you do engage with it. The way to advance in life is to make choices consistent with the inner law of your being. In the words of *The I Ching:*

> If the individual acts consistently and is true to himself, he will find the way that is appropriate for him.

Because of the accessibility and universality of their imagery, tarot cards are one useful means of assisting you to contemplate the forces operating in your life at any given moment. You can, therefore, ask yourself why a particular card emerged for your consideration at this time? And even more important, why did you have this particular emotional response to the card at this particular moment? Does it contain the solution to the problem you seek? Does it offer an innate clarity and sense of certainty that makes you think you now have the answer you've been looking for? Or did it drop into your lap like a rotten fish, begging to be thrown back into the void. Each possibility contains valuable information and insight; each of these responses is equally valid. Only you can judge what is true for you.

Synchronicity is a challenging concept to many of us—particularly those of us who have been schooled to rely exclusively on our rational cognitive processes to solve our problems. To engage in this hour's processes, whether through the tool of divination I have just shared with you or the other three related processes that will be introduced to you shortly, you will have to ask yourself a fundamental question, a question implicit in our consideration of the very notion: Do you think that this is a universe in which order is the norm and chaos the exception? Or do you believe that this is a basically chaotic universe with order an occasional accidental coincidence? Any discussion of divination is predicated on the assumption that you have bought into the concept that there is an unseen order to the universe supportive of your spiritual evolution and your expanding capacity to make good decisions. When you are in alignment with this unseen order, you have what the Jews call *mazel*

—luck, which means, in Hasidic tradition, "an influencing configuration of higher forces." Albert Einstein once said that the only question it is imperative for every human to ask of himself or herself is *whether this universe is friendly—or not?*

Synchronicity forces us to confront the question of the universe's inherently chaotic or orderly nature, with all the attendant implications. But before we proceed, I feel compelled to address an even more challenging aspect of the concept of synchronicity that ironically occurs exclusively among those who are most prone to optimism. I call it the Parking Space Syndrome.

Recently, Lisha, one of the cheeriest of my fellow explorers on the road less traveled, came to visit from San Francisco. Back in the *old* days, the early seventies and eighties, she and I had gotten involved in various positive-thinking practices that taught us that if we put ourselves in alignment with the universe we could be powerful. The entry into this new world of power was parking spaces. If you were aligned with the universe, the philosophy went, you could create parking spaces. This was no small miracle in San Francisco circa 1985 and so it was that we all went around mentally aligning ourselves to the universe and preparing our wills to manifest that most coveted of spiritual treasures: a cheap and legal place to dump the car.

In the subsequent years of living, having aligned myself to the universe to my satisfaction and having the attendant expected parking space fail to materialize on more than one occasion, I was confronted with a choice. Either I hadn't aligned myself to the universe well enough—or the parking space god was a bunch of hooey. Thanks to a well-timed Twelve-Step program I attended around that time, I encountered the concepts of acceptance and surrender in just the nick of time. I found the acceptance of human limitation to be a much healthier investment in my spiritual life than the creation of parking spaces, so I thought I'd forgotten all about magic. Then

Lisha arrived in Nashville. Our day's adventures featured a visit to Vanderbilt Divinity School. As we approached the campus parking lot, I commented offhandedly that because we were later than usual, we would never find a space. In the many months since I'd begun school, whenever I arrived at this hour, there had never been a space available. Lisha laughed at me. "Don't worry," she said in a suddenly irritating voice. "We'll create one."

Infinitely superior in my mature relationship to surrender, I set out to prove her wrong. Of course she wouldn't find a spot. But to my chagrin, a great parking space suddenly opened up directly in front of us.

It was a fluke, I reassured myself.

But the next day, the same thing happened. And the day after that. My core beliefs were shattered. I was angry and confused. Had I prematurely given up on making miracles happen in my life?

The day Lisha left, I approached the parking lot with trepidation —equally fearful that there would be a space waiting for me and that there would not be one. I did not want to take the destructive illusion of power and control back into my life—but I did want and deserve a good parking space as much as the next guy. Then suddenly a thought occurred to me. Instead of accepting that there would not be a parking space—and instead of assuming that I could create one—I would make my desires known to the universe and then accept whatever came. Guess what. Some days there is a parking space. Some days there is not. But whether a spot materializes or not, my daily search for a space has transformed into an adventure in which *anything is possible.*

Where I had once misunderstood power, I had more recently misunderstood acceptance. You have the right to a relationship with the universe that makes sense of your life. You have the right to ask for and hope for what you want. When you are in alignment with the unseen powers of the universe—when you can approach life's challenges with your enthusiasm, your moral integrity, and your vitality intact—you still cannot guarantee any particular result. However, you will be gifted with something just as valuable: You will intuitively trust that any of the seemingly bad things that happen to you are more likely to come from *outside* of you than to be contributed to or self-generated by either your own resistance or your own arrogance. Because the bad things are external to you, they will pass on again.

There are no guarantees, but it has been my experience that when one is driven by life, the odds are with you. You must set your intention as if this is an orderly, caring universe—and then be willing to engage with whatever arises. There is an order to the universe—the promise that in the end what is vitally good and right will prevail. Maybe not in your own time—but certainly in God's.

Of course you can not prove this rationally. When you hear the incessant reports of violence and war on the nightly news, you may be tempted to drop your prejudice in favor of order and surrender against the backdrop of mounting statistics. The philosopher Joseph Ernest Renan as quoted by William James advised his contemporaries:

> *In utrumque paratus,* then. Be ready for anything—that perhaps is wisdom. Give ourselves up, according to the hour, to confidence, to skepticism, to optimism, to irony, and we may be sure that at certain moments, at least, we shall be with the truth.

✳ Process: *Thunderstruck*

During this hour, you are going to ask four specific questions about the problem you would like to resolve by sunset. After formulating the questions in your own words, with all the attendant feelings and thoughts, you will release each question to the universe, trusting that the answer will come to you in its own time and in its own way.

The questions are these:

1. **What is the truth about the problem or issue I am facing in my life right now?**

2. **What is the nature of the obstacle that is in the way of resolving this problem by sunset tonight?**

3. **What should I do?**

4. **What outcome can I expect?**

You will have four tools from which to choose to assist you in this process. You can decide in advance to use one tool with all four questions; a different tool for each; or make up any combination as you go along, intuitively selecting whichever tool feels best and right at the moment. If this happens to be the summer solstice, or any day or situation where you have extra hours between now and sunset, you may want to stretch this process out longer than an hour. You could, if you so desire, spend as long as one hour on any of the four tools and questions.

✳ You have already been primed on the first tool: divination. You can use whatever form of divination you feel comfortable with—as long as you follow the guidelines I suggested to you earlier.

✳ A variation on this first tool comprises your second option: You may go to a favorite book, perhaps the Bible or some other spiritual work, and with question(s) in mind, open it at random and begin to read for guidance and meaning.

✳ The third tool guides you to take your question(s) for a walk in nature. As you stroll, remain receptive to personally meaningful signs in the environment—it may be a brave new sprout growing out of the blackened stump of a badly burned tree or a bluebird that alights nearby chirping a message that seems meant for you. Be open to anything that catches your eye and speaks to you metaphorically (or perhaps even literally). The teaching may come right away, or it may take some time. I once attended a workshop in which a participant reported that in the midst of his sacred process he had been frustrated to feel a call of nature. Grumbling, he made his way to the privvy for what he thought was going to be an unwelcome distraction. Instead, he stumbled upon the answer to his question. It was somehow mysteriously involved with the action of flushing the toilet. He reported to us that he had spent the greater part of his hour pulling the cord and watching the water swirl away, to some private, mystical end that resolved his problem to his utter and complete satisfaction.

✳ The fourth tool is to take your question into a closed-eyes meditation, or perhaps even into a deep sleep (don't forget to set your alarm). Ask for a vision or a dream to come to you with the answer you are hoping to receive. Dreams, according to Jungian psychology, are the voice of the unconscious, leading the conscious mind back to its sacred roots. If you choose this option, set your alarm to wake you in an hour. Have pen and paper right next to where you are napping. Immediately upon awakening, write down any dream images that came to you in as much detail as possible. At this juncture, they don't need to make any sense—or even apply to your issue.

✳ If you awaken without having had a dream, or instead choose to stay conscious during this process, you may have, in the place of a dream, a guided visualization. You can lead yourself through a visualization by closing your eyes and envisioning yourself in a beautiful place in nature, with a wise being walking toward you. The being can have a specific shape or form—it could even be someone

you have known in your life. Or it can be an energy form or a
feeling. However you imagine this being, it is bringing you a present.
What is it? If the present is in a box, open the lid and see what is
inside. Imagine this scene in as much detail as possible. You don't,
at this point, need to understand what the gift means. Simply accept
the present, thank the being, and then watch the being move off
into the distance. When the encounter is complete, open your eyes
and write down your experience in as much detail as possible. If the
gift is an object, you might want to try drawing a picture of it. When
you have finished this process, we will proceed.

Ten

No Choice

One hears—one does not seek; one takes—one does not ask who gives; a thought suddenly flashes up like lightning, it comes with necessity, unhesitatingly—I have never had any choice in the matter.
—*Nietzsche*

Did you get the answer you would have hoped for? Did you receive signs that are confusing or even unsettling? Did you apparently get nothing? In the next section, we will engage in a process that will help you make sense of the experiences that took place for you during this hour, regardless of the result you think you have or have not gotten. Remember, in the *Solved by Sunset* process there are no dead ends, nothing wasted. Soon you will crest and, with one final drop, flow over the top, transformed into a river, free to continue on your journey, the obstacle that seemed so insurmountable, now so easily overcome.

But before we move on to the next hour's teaching, I want to take a moment to share two experiences of the Thunderstruck process with you.

The first experience happened to a client of ours, the managing partner of a small San Francisco law firm. The last time I'd met with him, he was all business—no time for the pleasantries that can make even a demanding business environment tolerable. He was one of those guys who believes that business is war and that the way to succeed is to run your firm like an army. His employees and associates were carefully trained to do what he said without question. Consequently, while there was very little apparent dissension among the troops on a day-to-day basis, there was also high turnover in the firm. In fact, that was why he had called us in. He felt he needed to improve the firm's image in order to attract a higher caliber of employee.

I left his office determined to come up with a plan for him— although I had a sinking suspicion that public relations would be doing little more than putting adhesive tape over a hole in the hull of a sinking ship. But when I returned to see him some weeks later, plan in tow, he was a changed man.

As he told it, after our meeting he had stumbled into a particularly bleak crisis. One of his key people had left, taking several staff members and a big bite of business with her. Distraught, he had succumbed to the wishes of his wife to attend a day's spiritual retreat in the country where he would be required to spend the afternoon looking for a "teacher"—some aspect of nature that contained a lesson for him. Resistant to the notion, he'd stomped onto the retreat grounds certain that he was wasting his time and his money. Birds. Flowers. Feh. He sat on a rock, drawing pictures with a stick in the dirt, when suddenly he heard the sound of thundering hooves coming closer to him. Out of the brush that surrounded the manicured grounds came a family of deer. The four feisty animals, led by a magnificent buck, charged through the grounds with complete, unrestrained joy. They were not relating to one another out of obedience—but out of choice. There was nobody forcing them to stay together: they chose to stay together because they wanted to be with one another.

Out of this moment's revelation, he decided that he could and would begin to take time for pleasantries at the office. He arranged a luncheon at a favorite restaurant for his key people and surprised the office staff by bringing bunches of flowers to them for no particular reason. While we proceeded with our image-development campaign, it was no longer needed to attract a better class of associate, for turnover had ground to a halt. Instead, he asked us to direct our campaign toward attracting new clients. Before long, he was running one of the hottest firms in town.

People who heard his story started to send him buck mascots. There were stuffed fake deer, bucks carved from wood and out of stone. He ended up with deer ties and buck T-shirts. In the shamanistic tradition of certain Native Americans, one would say that this man had found his sacred animal guide—his totem.

I thought enviously of our client's buck when, some months afterward, Dan and I had the opportunity to drive through Sedona while doing business in Arizona. We had heard a great deal about energy vortexes and other mystical power centers—places that held the promise of assisting you in aligning your energy with the unseen order of the universe. We wanted to try it for ourselves, but with just several hours in town and no time to research the exact locations of the vortexes, we resorted to hiring a guide to take us into the red rock desert terrain to have our custom-ordered experience.

The tour guide was pleasant and helpful, although Dan and I felt more than a little foolish paying the fare for spirituality on demand. Luckily, we did not approach the experience with high expectations. Our carefree attitude, I'm certain, was fueled in part by the fact that we had no pressing issues on our minds that day. We could afford to be cavalier about the adventure.

As we arranged our tour in downtown Sedona, Dan and I were

presented with a sampling of spiritual options. Dan chose an encounter with a medicine wheel. I selected a meeting with my own personal totem animal. Finding the animal that would be important to me, that would protect and guide me, was something I had always wondered about and wished for. And so it was that I ordered up option number three from the list of possibilities. The guide drove us in a colorful Jeep out beyond the boundaries of the city of Sedona and to the foot of a glorious red rock cliff. Dan set off with our guide toward the sacred medicine wheel site, while I was told that I would have an hour during which a sacred encounter with my totem animal would transpire.

Left all alone, trudging through the scrubby underbrush, I walked with an air of expectancy. Was there the sound of a coyote howling in my future? The soaring of a magnificent hawk through the billowing clouds overhead? A buck charging into my heart? Nothing. Then the thought occurred to me: Of course, I am meant to have a vision, not a literal encounter. Feeling quite smug at having figured this out, I sat down in lotus posture and waited for something wonderful to happen. For the next several, long, minutes, a series of animals paraded through my thoughts one after another like oversize balloons winding their way down Fifth Avenue during the Macy's Thanksgiving Day parade. Tigers, bears, lions, dolphins—as soon as one made its hopeful appearance in my mind, another magnificent creature would bump it out of place to take its turn before the reviewing stand. After several painfully long minutes of this, I gave up—disgusted by my foolishness and opened my eyes. At that very moment, to my absolute horror, my eyes fell immediately upon a big, fat, pink worm crawling toward my right foot. It wasn't just any worm. I knew, without a doubt, that this was *my* worm. It lay there in the middle of the sandy desert terrain, ridiculously pink and squirmy. I've had years to think about the metaphysical significance of this worm (I won't bore you with this; however, suffice it to say

I've made peace with the idea that a worm turned out to be my sacred totem).

I was clear that this worm was significant to me. I could trust the message. But things are not always this clear. Do you always know whether the message or teaching you are receiving is true? How do you know when to keep the card and when to throw it back? When to accept the sign and when to dismiss it as ridiculous? Whether the resolution you've come up with will stick—and whether it won't? This is an issue that has been on the minds of spiritual seekers since the beginning of recorded history. And it is to this important subject that we will next turn our attention in the fifth hour of the *Solved by Sunset* process.

Different
Voices

Eleven

How Do You Know Which Voice Is Real?

If I'm deceived, Lord, it is by Thee.
—St. Augustine

The elegant woman stood before her fellow seminar participants, tears streaming down her cheeks. For several days, the woman had been incredibly self-contained, barely saying a word to anyone —certainly never showing any emotion. But during the fourth hour's exercise, she had pulled a card from the tarot deck picturing a stained-glass church window of a mother standing protectively beside her child. As she told the story to us between sobs, she explained how she and her daughter, who had converted to a fundamentalist faith, had become estranged over the issue of her religion. For several years, the mother had been refusing her daughter's calls and letters. She felt terrible about the situation. It was on her mind day and night. What should she do?

She reported to us that when she pulled that particular card, chills shot up her spine. She distinctly heard an inner voice telling her that it was time to reconcile, that she should finally make the call to her daughter. But as soon as she finished telling us the story, the tears stopped flowing. She got very quiet. The silence continued. And yet she went on standing mutely before us. What more was it she wanted to say?

The woman finally cleared her throat, dabbed at her eyes. Then, having somewhat regained her composure, shared the real reason she had volunteered to tell her moving story to us.

"I just needed to check out one thing—can I trust the voice? How do I know the voice I heard was telling me the truth?"

This is a fair question. Earlier, we addressed a similar question: Can you trust your emotions? The answer was no. You cannot trust your emotions to tell you the truth about reality. While your emotions have many other useful functions, providing trustworthy information about external circumstances is not one of them. So, how about your inner voice? Can you trust the voice within to tell you the truth—to really know what's best or right for you?

Even someone of the spiritual magnitude of St. Augustine had his doubts. Not even he could be sure that he was immune from being deceived by the voice he felt in every fiber of his being to be divine. He was far from the first spiritual leader to grapple with this question. Within the pages of the Bible, the issue is raised by the prophets themselves. For example, in the Book of Kings, God calls on the members of his inner circle, the Host of Heaven, to come up with a plan to tempt the Israelite King Ahab into mortal battle.

> A spirit came forward and stood before the LORD, saying, "I will entice him." "How?" the LORD asked him. He replied, "I will go out and be a lying spirit in the mouth of all his prophets."

Four hundred prophets, each of whom presumably felt truly called to speak God's word, were misled by a single deceiving spirit. To complicate the story even further, the deceiving spirit appears to have been commissioned by the prophets' very own God. That this story is part of the foundation of the Judeo-Christian tradition, demonstrates that this question—of whether you can trust your inner voice to guide you unfailingly into alignment with the unseen order—has been causing spiritual seekers anxiety since ancient times.

And for good reason. With so many groups claiming that they exclusively have the right to speak for God, who are you to trust? How are you to evaluate their claims? God speaks to the Jews in Israel and the Arabs in Palestine. God's voice tells one person when to pull the trigger, another when to give all her money to the church. Routinely, tourists on pilgrimages to Jerusalem wander away from their tour group only to turn up several days later draped in a bed-sheet issuing God's judgment.

On the personal level, the questions can be equally disturbing. Even if you received a clear answer to your inquiries in the previous exercise, can you know for sure that the voice you heard has your best interests in mind? Could it be your own subconscious undermining you because of unresolved guilt issues and the like? Could it be a deceiving spirit? Just whose voice was it that answered the four questions in the Thunderstruck exercise? Who wrote your myth? *Who is it who is reading and evaluating these very words?*

In the case of the seminar participant who stood before us, it was clear to all who observed her that she was a woman who had encountered her own higher truth through the tarot card and the inner voice. As she spoke aloud the voice's words to her, she was animated, present, fully alive. As she spoke her considerations, justi-fied as they were, she was dull, withdrawn, fearful. But it wasn't up to us to pass judgment on the validity of her inner experience. That she could only do for herself. Rather than offer my opinion, I asked her what it had felt like to her that instant when she felt she knew what she must do.

"I had this moment when everything seemed clear to me. And then, there were goose bumps all up and down my body." As she told about the goose bumps her composure once again cracked and she began to laugh.

"Goose bumps are a good sign," she finally managed to choke out through her giggles. "Every time a thought gives me goose bumps, whether I like it or not, it turns out to be the right thing for me to do." Her doubts passed and she was reconnected to her sense that what she had felt directed to do was the right thing for her. She returned to her seat, eager for the next break so that she could make the call to her daughter.

This woman had a felt sense of the rightness of the voice's information for her. But as St. Augustine and the 400 prophets illustrate, it is not always so clear. You not only have the right, but the obligation to bring a critical objectivity to messages you receive inwardly, either from your own unconscious and/or from the divine. Happily, there is a way you can test your inner voice for authenticity. Before we are through with this hour's process, you will have what I believe is the best possible way to evaluate the information you receive. You will also be given a process by which you will be able to use your inner voice to help you evaluate messages delivered to you by others who claim their sources to be divinely inspired. As a result, you will be less fearful of being deceived and more certain about whether the voice you have tuned in to is offering the best advice.

By now, you are undoubtedly beginning to recognize that the complexities and dynamics of what is transpiring inside of you every moment of every day can be as fascinating and challenging as your outer circumstances. If you have been involved in psychological processes, such as therapy, or spiritual practices, such as meditation, you have already begun to familiarize yourself with the challenging territory that lies within your mind and spirit. However, it is also true that you are probably still distracted by the need to make a success of yourself in the world and that you are able and willing to put your more contemplative, apparently less productive spiritual practices on the back burner when they become inconvenient or distracting.

Perhaps part of your reluctance to make the time to do the kind of inner work prescribed in this book on a regular basis comes from the suspicion that there may be some voices inside of you that you would rather not hang out with more than is absolutely necessary. A jealous voice, a greedy one, a lazy one. And worse. We all have these darker voices within us. We also have wise and knowing voices—but even these we would sometimes rather not listen to because we have the sneaky suspicion that they may very well be trying to get a message through to us we'd rather not heed. For instance, what if the voice you encountered in the last process is asking you to do something that will shake up the comfort of the status quo—to take a risk—in order to serve a higher purpose in your life? Or what if the voice is telling you that you can't have what you think you want; or that you don't really want what you have worked so hard to achieve? You want to resolve your problem by sunset tonight—there's a voice in you right now ready to tell you exactly how to go about this, how to get the resolution you are seeking. The only reason you haven't resolved your problem yet (if you haven't) is because you are not listening to what this voice is telling you to do. You are arguing with it or ignoring it because you don't want to do what the voice says is the thing you have to do in order to grow.

An expert on the subject of avoidance is independent floor trader Edward Allen Toppel, who has spent nearly twenty years in the S&P futures pit in the Chicago Mercantile Exchange. On the very day Toppel made some of his greatest profits trading IBM options, he had an enlightening experience, which formed the basis of his book *Zen in the Markets: Confessions of a Samurai Trader*.

The crux of what he discovered is this: There are only four rules of trading and investing if you want to make money on the stock exchange. "1. Buy low, sell high. 2. Let profits run, cut losses quickly. 3. Add to a winning position, not a loser. 4. Go with the trend."

Sounds easy. So why is it that so many people play the stock market and end up losing big-time? Toppel explains that people ignore their inner voice of wisdom that knows these rules, tuning in, instead, to the ego-driven voices of pride, greed, guilt, shame, fear, and the like. According to Toppel, the trouble begins when we take a position in the market and it doesn't become an instant winner.

> Ego starts to tighten its grip over our ability to do the right thing. The right thing is to get rid of our losers immediately. The ego will produce the most fantastic reasons for holding on to that money-draining position, be it in stocks, bonds, options, or futures. Ego will fight us all the way and prevent us from realizing quickly that it is better to swallow our pride and do the right thing.

Toppel goes on to explain that when he was a broker with Bear, Stearns, the ego-driven thinking among some of his clients was that you don't have a loss until you take it. "They would hang on until the market proved they were right. How ridiculous and how very expensive it was for some of them."

Many of us work hard not to hear the voice of wisdom that always knows what's best for us. It was such a voice that whispered to me for years leading up to the purchase of our "dream" home some fourteen years ago. The voice whispered insistently that the prize would not be worth the sacrifice. I knew, in my heart, that when I finally got the big house in the right suburb, overlooking San Francisco Bay, Dan and I would never have the opportunity to spend time in it—we would be too busy working all hours to pay the mortgage. The fantasy I had of romping with my young children on the rolling lawns would belong to the nanny I would have to hire—not to me. But the more Dan and I threw our weight around with realtors and bankers, feeling the surge of power that generates from the momentum of pursuing and obtaining a house beyond your means, the less able I was to admit to the presence of this "disloyal" little voice—least of all to myself.

If you ignore voices of wisdom long enough, inevitably you end up in trouble. Virtually the moment we signed the mortgage, we began to sink financially. Eventually, our debt load and attendant work schedules got so out of hand I was forced to admit to the authenticity of the voice that had been warning me against our decision and that was now telling me to get us out of it as quickly as possible. I finally listened, despite the fact that as a result I was forced to spend several alternately terrifying and ebullient years white-knuckling it through the ups and downs of financial, emotional, and spiritual recovery. I now try very hard to override my ego and listen to my inner voice of wisdom earlier. By so doing I can usually get out of whatever mess I'm heading for in a more timely manner so that the recovery time will not be as massive or painful as it was the first time around. As *The I Ching* comforts those of us who have managed to ignore or argue with our own inner wisdom, we can thank heavens that "Life moves upward and lets the mistakes sink down behind it."

One of the ways we avoid having to tune into our inner knowing is by staying so busy that uncomfortable thoughts can't break through to our consciousness. Have you noticed how many highly successful people have difficulty when things get too quiet around them? Why, if faced with enforced inactivity do you react with such anxiety and impatience? How many ambitious people do you know who routinely avoid peaceful vacations, such as sitting with a good book on an isolated island beach, in favor of attending a competitive tennis camp or hitting ten European cities in twelve days? The other day, my friend Donna and I were savoring our cherished moments of serene friendship walking the unpaved paths around Radnor Lake, when we stumbled upon an executive putting in her hour's exercise in nature while making deals on her mobile cellular phone!

I believe people do this to themselves because when they stop providing new input at the level of the noisy activity and performance of their everyday lives, their inner voices have the opportunity to be heard. We think we are clever at avoiding our internal moment of reckoning, but the truth is, if we don't allow our inner voices to rise to consciousness they will make themselves known to us in the form of problems. Since external events are guaranteed to get our attention—*a problem like the one you are working with today*—that is exactly what we get. Even if it's painful to hear what the voice is telling you, wouldn't you rather know what you are really dealing with in your life earlier on, when you will be more likely to do something about it, than to be overtaken again and again by "bad luck" and unwelcome surprises?

Soon, you are going to have the opportunity not only to get to know your inner voice of wisdom—a voice you can count on to be on your side—but to know all the voices that populate your inner constellation.

We've been referring to "voices" on and off since early this morning. The word *voices* is a poetic description, a psycho-spiritual device to give you a way to think of your inner experience. You may prefer to think of these voices as aspects of yourself or divine knowledge and wisdom or unconscious influences—such as the things you were taught in school, the ways your parents thought about the world, and so on—or the possibility I believe to be most likely, some combination of these. However you think about these communications, the goal is to identify and engage each of the voices within you in productive dialogue: helping them to work with one another to address challenges and conflicts—both internal and external; to explore the new frontiers of your creativity and intuition; and simply to enjoy getting to know and appreciate the miracle of all that you are.

You may think this whole discussion about voices is nutty—something more applicable to people in the psychiatric ward than to you. Think again. The voices are in you and have been all your life. If you don't believe me, let's say you are about to do something you're sure is wrong—you know better. *Who is it that knows it's wrong?* Perhaps you've thought of that voice as your conscience. I call that voice our Higher Self. By Higher Self, I mean that it is a part of you that has expanded perspective, greater awareness, and that can be counted on to watch out for your well-being. It is the voice that you can trust to point out the way that will bring you into alignment with the unseen order of the universe. I don't always choose to listen to my Higher Self, but I know it is always available to me, if I am willing to put aside my left-brain I-can-do-it-myself ego long enough to ask for help.

Now let's take a look at another occasion that calls forth a very different voice in you. There are those times when you try to do something and fall short of your goal. You know you could have done better and you feel badly about it. Who knows you could have done better? *Who tells you to feel bad?* This is the voice I call the Critic. You know you are dealing with the Critic when the words and tone remind you of your least favorite grammar school teacher, or any of those other adults who knew just how to "get" you when you were young. *"You're a loser. You'll never amount to anything. How could you be so stupid?"* Nobody gets through their childhood without someone delivering this message to them on one or more unfortunately memorable occasions. Interestingly enough, even the Critic's voice—misguided though it is—can, in its own way, be watching out for your well-being. The Critic is trying to keep you from experiencing more pain by trying to get you to give up before you make a real fool of yourself. If you hear it from your inner voice first, you may be saved from having to hear it from the outside world later. The Critic may be well-meaning—or not. But in any case, the voice of harsh self-judgment does not have to be the only voice we hear, even if it is often the loudest.

The Higher Self and the Critic are two of the major voices, but there are many more. You have an inner child in you. In fact, you probably have several. You may have a loving, playful child who comes out when you have dull work to do, tempting you to leave the dishes undone to go and dig in the garden. You may also have a whiny, needy child who didn't get enough love and attention when you were young, and who is still crying out to have his or her needs taken care of. You have dynamic go-getter voices in you— the goal-setters and achievers, and you have dreamy, intuitive voices —spiritual caretakers and mystics. Your inner life is as rich and diverse as a pantheon of Greek gods and goddesses. In fact, mythology and legend—many psychologists believe—may well be the expression of the inner world made visible through story and art. As the philosopher Rollo May contends, in ancient Greece:

> . . . When the myths were vital and strong, individuals in the society were able to meet the problems of existence without overwhelming anxiety or guilty feelings. Hence we find the philosophers in those times discussing beauty, truth, goodness, and courage as values in human life. The myths freed Plato and Aeschylus and Sophocles to create their great philosophic and literary works, which come down as treasures for us today.

During this, the fifth hour's process, you will discover that some of the voices you encounter will appeal to you; some may repel you at first. Interestingly enough, the voices also have opinions about each other. Are you suffering from inner conflict—torn between options? Perhaps the stress is being caused by disparate voices fighting with one another for your attention? For example, your secretary asks you for a raise he doesn't deserve, and you are upset and confused about what to do. Loving inner child says yes! But inner child always wants to give to others. Critic says if you do give the raise, you're being taken again. But you know you can always count on critic to speak your worst fears.

Or maybe you are thinking about changing careers. Your dynamic doer is urging you to take the risk! Go for it! While needy inner child is scared out of her wits at the prospect. The dreamy goddess would just as soon quit entirely and spend her days in contemplation. So many voices competing for your attention!

The question is not how to be rid of all the chatter that is going on incessantly in your mind and spirit, but whether you would like to have some say about which voices are worth listening to; whether your inner dialogue will go on unconsciously, influencing your decisions without your active participation; or if you are instead willing to engage consciously in the process of embracing as much of your authentic self as possible. When there are problems in your inner or outer world, must the voices be locked in combat with each other —or can you call on your Higher Self, your God-given ability to judge and discriminate, to mediate and find compromises, that will help you toward resolution? Is there a voice that can hear all the others out and then make a balanced decision that will be best for all of the voices? Because you will soon have a means of identifying the voices within you, you can be less fearful about the prospect of being deceived and more certain about which is offering you the best advice. Before we are through with this hour's process, you will have the tools not only to evaluate inwardly received information, but a way to turn to your inner voices to help you evaluate messages delivered to you by others who may or may not be as discriminating about the authenticity of the voices they are tuning in as you will soon be about your own.

Twelve

Your Personal Board of Directors

Sometime during the course of this day, one or more of your inner voices has been operative inside of you. If you have already resolved your problem, chances are that you were able to tune in to a voice that offered you insight and guidance that you intuitively knew to be true for you. A second possibility is that the voice or voices you connected with have provided you with information and advice you aren't sure how to evaluate. If neither of the previous scenarios is true for you, and you are beginning to believe that you are the one person in the world who doesn't have a Higher Self to tap into and that you are a fool for having invested this time and purchased this book, chances are that the voice that has been calling the shots for you today is your inner critic.

During this fifth-hour process, a writing exercise, you will have the opportunity to familiarize yourself with the key voice or voices that you have been in communication with today—as well as a few that have been operating quietly behind the scenes, unbeknownst to you. You will then be able to engage these voices in productive dialogue.

✳ Process: *Dialogue with Your Inner Voices*

It is time now to find a comfortable place where you will be able to write undisturbed for about an hour. When you are settled, read through the rest of this exercise, following the instructions as they are given.

✳ To begin the process, it will be helpful for you to think of your voices as an internal board of directors. As in most companies, the board gets together on a regular basis to consider issues pertinent to the successful operation of the organization. In this case, that organization happens to be you. When challenging problems, decisions or issues come up, and disparate opinions are likely to be voiced by individuals representing various points of view who will lobby more or less successfully for their position. If the board is well managed, there will be someone who facilitates the voices fairly, making sure each of the members is heard and respected. The voices will be encouraged to dialogue with one another, with the ultimate goal of reaching a consensus. Not everyone participating may be pleased with every decision or agree with every aspect—in fact, many groups have their own special curmudgeon whose sole role it seems is to hold and express the most disagreeable point of view. But in a healthy process, there is general agreement that for the good of the company as a whole, individual positions may and can be softened to accommodate the group wisdom as to the best course of action.

Today, you are going to bring the problem you would like to resolve by sunset before your inner board of directors and ask them to reach a consensus on what will work best for you. If you already have a solution to your problem, or have received a dominant communication from one voice in particular, you are going to ask that board member to speak up first. If not, the Critic will be the kick-off speaker. The gavel is in your hand. Imagine the voices filing into the inner boardroom of your dreams: Perhaps it resembles the U.S. Senate chambers, a cozy retreat center, or the headquarters for IBM. You are going to write down both your questions and comments, including your opening statements—which I will be giving to you shortly in boldface print—and your board members' spontaneous responses. *Any directions or comments I want to share with you that you don't have to write down will be in italics.* Take about five minutes per response, allowing each board member in turn to speak whatever comes into your mind. As in the first hour's process when you originally set your intentions for the day, write nonstop, as fast as you can. Don't lead your thoughts—follow them. If nothing comes to mind, write that "nothing comes to mind." If you are stuck for something to write, or feel as if you can't move your willful, goal-setting rational mind out of the way, switch your pen to your less dominant hand. Let mistakes go uncorrected. It's time at last to call the meeting to order and to call on your first speaker.

Will the first voice please tell us: What position have you taken in relation to the problem I want to solve by sunset? Do you have some satisfying resolution in mind? If so, what is it? If not —what's getting in the way?
Copy these opening questions on your paper then continue with the first voice's response. Allow this speaker to name him or herself: is it Higher Self? Critic? Steadfast Tin Soldier? When you have written five minutes or so, give all of your other board members the opportunity to express their opinions.

What does Critic have to say about this?

What does the nurturing voice have to say about this?

What does the inner child have to say about this?

Is there anybody else who would like to offer his or her opinion at this time, about any of the previous speakers—or about my role as chairman of the board?

Keep asking this last question and recording the responses until every board member present has had the opportunity to speak what's on his or her mind. When everybody has spoken, continue with the next instruction.

It's time for us to hear from our special counsel, Higher Self *(again, if Higher Self has already spoken).* Higher Self, having heard all these voices, what is your opinion now? If you previously sent me a sign, symbol, or dream image I did not fully understand, now is the time to reveal to me the significance of it. What does it mean? What guidance are you trying to give to me?

Higher Self carries the wisdom for the board: the voice of vision tempered by experience. Higher Self has the presence of mind to help you discern the various contributions each of the other voices on the board are capable of making.

After Higher Self has spoken, ask yourself whether consensus has been reached. Have all the board members acceded to Higher Self's guidance? If so, you may call this session of the board of directors to its conclusion.

If you have not come to a resolution, you are going to open the floor for discussion. Begin with the loudest, strongest, or most irritating voice. If this is its first appearance, ask for his or her name. Let each of the voices already identified—or any new voice that wants to enter the debate—tell whomever they please what they think of you, them, or their idea. If you are having trouble differentiating between voices, use your dominant hand for your strong voices and your recessive hand for your weaker ones. As the convener of the board, you or Higher Self can intercede whenever necessary to make sure that the voices are being respectful to their fellow board members—whether or not they agree with one another. If you feel you would like an example of this exercise before you try it, you may take a moment at this point to read ahead to the ''Dialogue with Your Inner Voices'' sample that follows, giving you a sense of how multiple voices might work together toward consensus.

When you are finished with this process—either by coming to consensus or realizing that, for the time being, consensus does not appear to be possible —conclude with the following statement:

Board Members, Higher Self, I would like to thank you for your time and trouble on this matter. Meeting adjourned.

✳ *Sample Dialogue with Your Inner Voices*

Will the first speaker please tell us: What position have you taken in relation to the problem I want to solve by sunset? Do you have some satisfying resolution in mind? If so, what is it? If not—what's getting in the way?
I can't think of a thing to say. I feel too guilty about taking time away from the office to be concentrating on this stupid exercise right now. Am I doing the right thing to be trying to solve my problem this new way? I've heard this voice before. I must be Worry Wart. I'm careful and conscientious. I'm a lot like your big sister, Katy. She worried a lot about you, too. I think my job must be to keep you safe.

What does Critic have to say about this?
I'm sick and tired of stupid Worry Wart. He thinks he's just like his big sister, Katy. But that's not true. He's nowhere as well-meaning as she was. He's just a great, big lazy good-for-nothing, looking for any excuse for you not to do your job. You're just looking for excuses, like always. I'm Critic and proud of it. I tell the truth about

things, even if it hurts. I'm a lot like your grammar school principal was—on a bad day. You might not like the things I have to say, but I have an important job to do. I make sure you stay on the straight and narrow and don't get into any more trouble than you can handle.

What does Nurturer have to say about this?

I think Critic is being terribly unfair to Worry Wart and to you. All Worry Wart wants to do is protect you. I think you should shut Critic up and just go ahead and do the exercise. Of course you are doing the right thing; you always do the right thing. You are brave and wonderful taking time away from the office to try a new way of doing things. The problem you have on your mind today is very important. I say we stop this silly squabbling and address the issue you hope to resolve by sunset. You'll know just what to do.

What does the inner child have to say about this?

I agree with Nurturer, but I think we should take a break first. I'm the fun-loving Child, and I think it's such a great afternoon, and we had so much fun last hour walking in the woods, we should try it again. I know we forgot to get the assignment done—not a single sign or teaching. Oh well. Maybe we'll do better this time.

Is there anybody else who would like to register his or her opinion at this time?

If not, it's time for us to hear from our special counsel, Higher Self. Higher Self, having heard all these voices, what is your opinion now? If you previously sent me a sign, symbol, or dream image I did not fully understand, now is the time to reveal to me the significance of it. What does it mean? What guidance are you trying to give to me?

While I love Child's suggestion, I don't think that Child is old enough to be entrusted with the responsibility of getting this issue resolved by sunset. It will take all of us working together—and I know we do not do our best work outdoors. It's too distracting. I suggest we stay here together by the fireplace and work this through to consensus. I think it's possible. That's why I sent you that dream image. Remember, you were confused about it at the time. But now it will make sense to you. You dreamed you were drowning in deep water, but then suddenly your toes touched bottom. You realized you were in shallow water. All you had to do was stand up. You've been thinking this is a huge problem, but it's really not. We're really much closer to one another than you thought—and the solution is much closer to the surface than you thought. Worry Wart, I can see you really want to say something here. Go ahead.

Worry Wart: I'm not so sure we have so much in common and that this will be so easily solved just by standing up. What critic said before really hurt my feelings. I am not a lazy, good-for-nothing. Why do you always want to hurt me? I just can't go on the way things have been. I'm not lazy. I just need a little bit of time to sort things out. Why won't you lighten up on me?

Critic: If I lightened up on you, you'd just go and waste your life, playing and goofing around with Child like you did in the last process.

Nurturer: Playing and goofing around would be good for Worry Wart. Great, in fact. But that's not who I think is talking right now. I think who's really talking is the Vulnerable Voice—the voice that Worry Wart is trying to protect.

Vulnerable Voice: You're right. I'm grateful that Worry Wart takes such good care of me. But I think I've got to find a better way to do things. I don't really want to escape from my responsibilities.

Critic: I don't believe you.

Vulnerable Voice: If I got Higher Self to confirm that I'm telling the truth, would you listen?

Critic: Maybe.

Higher Self: Vulnerable Voice is telling the truth. She's a part of you that's crying out for help. She isn't lazy. In fact, she's working very hard right now—just not in the way you're used to.

Unidentified Voice: You're getting taken in, Higher Self. Critic's right. Sitting here scribbling nonsense—when she could be at the office working. It's unproductive.

Higher Self: Who are you?

Unidentified Voice: I'm Dynamo, Critic's pal. I'm the one who watches out for your welfare. I get us to the office to make money. If I had my way, we'd be working eighty-hour weeks. Without me, you'd fail.

Second Unidentified Voice: That's not true. My name is Recovering Superwoman. I'm the one who bought this book. I used to work eighty-hour weeks—just like Dynamo would like to do. But remember where it got us? We got sick. In fact, that's the reason we're here today. We're deciding what to do about the fact that I cut my hours back to a more reasonable forty to fifty hours a week —and became infinitely more productive. But the boss thinks I'm slacking off, just like Critic. You're both a bunch of idiots. Now I've got to figure out what to do. Do I go back to the old way of working eighty hours a week to look good for the boss—or do I quit?

Critic: You mean to say your productivity didn't drop at all?

Recovering Superwoman: Au contraire. I made more sales during the last quarter working normal hours than I ever did working that burn-out schedule my boss expects of me.

Dynamo: Does your boss know that? I bet if somebody told him, he'd get off your case.

Recovering Superwoman: Nah. He'd never go for it. He thinks it would set a bad example for the other sales reps.

Higher Self: But what if you asked to be taken off salary and put on commission?

Chairman: Hmm. Interesting idea. Sam asked for that several months ago and it's worked out great for him.

Critic: Yeah. But I know you. If you went on commission, you'd just play around with Child all the time. Get nothing done. We'd starve.

Child: I don't want to starve! Please, Recovering Superwoman, don't let me starve! I'll do anything!

Recovering Superwoman: Child, will you keep yourself busy during normal work hours so that I can earn us a living—if I promise, no fingers crossed, to play with you everyday when I get home from work?

Child: I promise.

Higher Self: So is that it? Do we all agree? Recovering Superwoman will ask the boss to go on commission and Child will leave her alone during work hours so that she can earn us a living. Is that okay with you, everyone?

Dynamo: Yo.

Nurturer: Whatever feels best to you, dear.

Vulnerable Voice: As long as you promise to take good care of me.

Worry Wart: I'm still not sure this is going to work, but what the hey, it's worth a try.

Higher Self: And how about you, Critic? You thought it was going to be a disaster when Recovering Superwoman cut her hours in the first place—and productivity went up. Dynamo, Worry Wart, Nurturer, Child, Critic—you all want what's best for our chairman. Can you agree to work together to keep Chairman on track? Don't you think you can trust one another to keep your agreements?

Critic: Well, maybe a little. But let it be known that I do not agree with this plan of action. However, since the board's decision has been reached taking my point of view into consideration, I will accede to the majority.

Higher Self: I appreciate your generosity of spirit, Critic. Tell you what. It's true that you've sometimes been right about things in the past. Perhaps we could try this out for just for one month or so. The Chairman can ask to go on commission on a temporary trial basis to make sure everybody is doing their part. If it doesn't work, she can always ask to go back on salary. Is that agreed?

All Voices in unison: Agreed.

Chairman: Board Members, Higher Self, I would like to thank you for your time and trouble on this matter. Meeting adjourned.

Thirteen

The Prophet Test

With this concluding chapter of hour number five, "Different Voices," we will revisit this section's original concern: How do you know which voice is real?

The immediate answer is: every one of your inner voices is "real." Each has a valid contribution to make—an important role to play. Through inner dialogue, the voices can be trusted to test one another, to challenge the various points of view they represent, and to work together to come to consensus. If you had a spontaneous breakthrough earlier today, you can test out the voice that brought you the information by submitting that voice to the process I have just shared with you. Chances are that if your insight is one that promises to bring you into closer alignment with the unseen order, it will stand the test of your toughest critic. If not, you may soon discover that what you thought was the perfect solution was little more than wishful thinking.

I remember, for example, one day shortly after I received my brown belt in karate. I'd gone from a white to an orange belt with unwavering commitment, which inspired my progress. Through karate, I discovered depths of self-discipline I did not know I had. I felt strong, grounded, and stable—physically as well as mentally and spiritually. Aided by the fact that Dan and I were studying together, karate had become very important to me in my life. But somewhere between orange and brown, I became pregnant. Suddenly what had seemed easy and inspired became difficult for me. The imperative was gone, but urged on by my sensei, I pushed my way through to brown—even with a timeout just long enough to give birth to Jody. But when I resumed classes after her birth, things did not go easier. Despite Dan's encouragement, it was more of a struggle than ever to keep myself motivated.

One day before class, feeling deeply conflicted, I took a long walk alone through the reedy path that bordered the bay near our Marin County home. I tuned in my inner voices as best I could—given that I didn't have the "Dialogue with Your Inner Voices" process to work with at the time. One voice in particular was speaking to me. The voice had such an authoritative feel to it, that I assumed it was of no less than divine origin. The voice told me that everybody gets into slumps from time to time. That the way out of this abyss was not to retreat, but to push forward. I should recommit myself to karate more than ever. I could go all the way with this—all the way to black belt. It was worth the price. And so, obediently, I did as the voice instructed.

For several weeks, I forced myself to leave Jody and Grant to practice. I showed up at class and, alongside Dan, gave my workout everything I had. But then one evening I caught a glimpse of myself in the dojo mirror—a shell of white karate uniform performing a *kata*. The uniform/the mirror/the form: I realized that I had become a ghost of images, mechanically performing a ritual act, rather than the vital practitioner of martial arts I knew I had the potential to be. Where had my spirit gone? Suddenly I knew without a shadow of a doubt that for the time being my spiritual growth was not in the practice of karate—at least not in the physical sense. Instead, I decided to apply what I had learned from my studies in karate to the more pressing area of my spiritual journey: motherhood. All of my karate practice had been to prepare me for this. Now it was time for me to leave karate behind and get on with my life. I would not pursue my black belt. As hard as it would be to watch Dan proceed with the class, eventually obtaining what had once been our mutual goal, I had to let it go. As I spoke with the sensei about my decision, my trepidation about his response melted beneath the waves of compassion, understanding, and humility I felt for myself. I had been pushing my way through my brown belt, based on the fear that if I quit before having attained black, I would lose everything. I didn't know then what I know now. That you can't lose what truly belongs to you—even if you throw it away.

But what of the voice I'd heard that day in the reeds? It had spoken with such authority. In the wake of my decision to quit, I recognized it finally as a voice I'd been listening to all my life: a voice that had taught me that growth must come through suffering and sacrifice and discipline. The voice I'd listened to that day was none other than my very own guilt. I had been giving myself permission to deny my self-nurturing instinct's own healthy impulse to pamper myself and my newborn child. My ego-driven emotions had muffled my ability to pick out the authentic voice of my higher consciousness. By allowing myself to give up the pursuit of a black belt in order to better care for myself and my children, was I experiencing growth or regression? For me, at that moment of my life, surrendering the wishful thinking of the imagined God-given payoffs of my mastery of karate and snuggling down to pay heed to my more prosaically human urge to nurture and love was the heroic path to take.

I did not have a process like the one I have just taught to you to help me familiarize myself with and differentiate between the various voices that hold court in my brain. Even so, I managed to make my way through the jumble of conflicting opinions that were rolling around clogging up my cognitive structures. While I'm glad I have a handy process to call upon when I am faced with inner conflict concerning issues such as this, I have resisted the notion that I have found a foolproof way to protect myself from life's often messy nature.

Do not take the voice dialogue process I shared with you in this section and use it to routinely distance yourself from letting your life unfold as it may, learning from your mistakes, trusting that sooner or later you will figure out which end is up. While you may want to use this process to some degree of excess for the time being, over time you will instinctively learn to recognize that you can take the risk of trusting your spontaneous insights without submitting them to any process more scientific than the "goose-bump" test that worked for the woman who chose to reconcile with her daughter.

But my little karate story, innocuous as it may be, leads us onto much trickier—and potentially even dangerous—spiritual turf. For as this story illustrates, just because one feels strongly that one is getting a clear and direct communication from the divine, does not necessarily mean that one has a grasp of the complete picture. We all have tendencies toward the grandiose. It is easy to use garden variety brushes with inner wisdom (or in the case of the story I just related, inner guilt) and blow them into the grandly expanded notion that one has been specially called to carry a message to the rest of planet Earth. I confess that both as a writer of spiritual literature and as a student of theology, this is either an ambition or a delusion that has on occasion been known to visit me.

But believing that God has guided you to go for your black belt, or even to write a piece of self-help literature, is only one magnitude of issue. Coming up against someone who believes that God has commissioned him to murder a doctor who works at a Planned Parenthood Clinic, or to join a cult, is quite another. If you feel specially chosen to deliver God's message to your fellow humans— or when you come into contact with someone who claims to be divinely inspired be they a channeler, a cultist, a revolutionary, an author, a politician, a talk-show host, or a tel-evangelist, you can start by testing out the authenticity of their message by submitting it to the scrutiny of your Board of Directors. Let that voice enter into dialogue with your own inner voices and you will have the tools you need to protect yourself from the seductive excitement of those whose intense conviction will attempt to sweep you into its field of gravity.

I hope and trust that as a result of our discussions and experiences over these past five processes, you will have a newfound respect and understanding of the complexities, implications, and import inherent in tapping into the wisdom (and pitfalls) of yours as well as other people's inner voices.

I would like you to use the gift of your insight and wisdom to consider the full implications of what it can mean to you to be freed from the limitations of left-brain rational thinking. Make this shift, and instead of living your life being driven by the urge to resolve your many problems as they arise, you will have but one overriding goal: to live your life as fully as possible, trusting that your problems will both be presented to you and resolved as a by-product of the growth of your character and your spirit.

Eleven
Questions

Fourteen

This Is Your Moment

There is, apart from mere intellect, in the makeup of every superior human identity, a wondrous something that realizes without argument . . . an intuition of the absolute balance, in time and space, of the whole of this multifariousness, this revel of fools, and incredible make-believe and general unsettledness, we call the world.

— *Walt Whitman*

I have promised you resolution by sunset. If you have not already had an epiphany, this is the hour and the process that can do it. It has happened for many, many people in my workshop sessions—it can happen for you.

There is, of course, a caveat. The *Solved by Sunset* process only works if you share the four assumptions we have been working with throughout this book. To refresh your memory, they are:

1. **There is an unseen order in the universe.**

2. **Your highest good lies in harmoniously adjusting yourself to this unseen order.**

3. **Whatever keeps you from experiencing your alignment with the universe is accidental, and can be overcome.**

4. **Forces beyond your comprehension are already engaged in your problem-solving process.**

If you complete this hour's work (and throw in the next and final hour's process for good measure) and still don't have the resolution you seek, the most likely explanation is that your unconsciously held beliefs are in conflict with the premises upon which this book is based. This is not a hopeless situation. In fact, it is a great gift to have found some way to dig through your illusions of what you think or wish you believed, to discover what it is you actually do believe. By bringing your unconscious programming to the surface, you can be in a position to make a decision about the assumptions that you want to keep—the ones to cast away—and the ones to adopt, which will determine how you will experience your life. The beliefs you keep will determine the nature of your spiritual life.

You don't get to have a say about whether or not you will be a spiritual person, by the way. We all have spiritual beliefs. Spirituality, according to *The American Heritage Dictionary,* is derived from the root word *spirit,* which means "the vital principle or animating force traditionally believed to be within living beings." The issue is not whether you are a spiritual being—of course there is a vital animating force within you. Rather, the real issue is how will the particular beliefs you hold, as a spiritual being, enhance or detract from your connection to the unseen powers of the universe? If you believe that human nature is essentially sinful, you will be drawn to old paradigms of external authority. If you believe that human beings are essentially good, you will be open to the kinds of processes you have been participating in today. Is this an "each man for himself" kind of world? Then your life will be like war. Or is human nature, when stripped of its fear-generated resistances, loving? If you believe the latter, then you are likely to find a place for good relationships and teamwork in your life. Like it or not, we all believe something. But when you hold your worldview unconsciously, you become the victim rather than the vehicle of those beliefs. You can bring your assumptions to consciousness through honesty and self-evaluation. You can choose to release those beliefs that no longer serve you, and to incorporate new, healthier beliefs into your consciousness.

Ralph Waldo Emerson contended that every individual has an essential choice to make: the choice between truth and repose. He who chooses repose

> . . . will accept the first creed, the first philosophy, the first political party he meets—most likely his father's. He gets rest, commodity, and reputation; but he shuts the door of truth. He in whom the love of truth predominates . . . submits to the inconvenience of suspense and imperfect opinion, but he is a candidate for truth, as the other is not.

Joseph Campbell, conversing with Bill Moyers in *The Power of Myth*, described beliefs as computer software. You program the computer with your beliefs, and the computer responds accordingly. If you don't like your results, change the programming. Even Joseph Campbell liked to play with the software, adding new ideas as they crossed his path, tossing away others he had outgrown.

If you have the suspicion that your software system could use a debugging, consider taking a break from the problem you initially chose to resolve today, and instead during this next process work with the issue of adopting a healthier, more productive belief system. Once this is in place, you can always apply this day's processes to the issue you originally set out to resolve—and on any problems that arise in the future. I believe you will discover that these processes will help you resolve whatever issues come up for you.

The reason I can say this with a real degree of certainty is because

I believe that there is a higher power pulling for you—a grander scheme in which your evolution plays a part. You would not be here today, with this problem on your mind, if an infinite number of miracles had not taken place already. Look at the moment of your conception. Billions of sperm had been released into a hostile environment, perhaps over and over again, competing among themselves to reach the goal of fertilization. Only one sperm succeeded. It took these improbable odds to create the exact configuration of physical, emotional, intellectual, and spiritual characteristics that are known as *you*. If another sperm had succeeded, if it had been another egg's turn, you would be a different person. And this did not only happen for you and your particular life, but for each of the parents who contributed to your birth, and to the parents that contributed to theirs and so on back into the deepest reaches of humanity's existence.

You have definite proof that over time, the actions of nature that promote life have a greater tendency to succeed than those that promote the suppression of life. How do you know that? Because you exist. The event of your presence and the occurrence of the world with which you interact is neither rational nor logical. Your very existence is deeply mysterious. You, and those who preceded you, survived war, plague, and holocaust in order for you to be sitting here, reading these words at this very moment. You are the most current expression of this mystery manifesting in space and time.

And now let me ask you, doesn't it make sense that this unseen order is supportive of those deeper qualities that will ensure the continued evolution of life on our planet—qualities like character, faith, acceptance, and love? This higher power may not care if you can close the sale on the particular house you want or get named president of the corporation. But the unseen powers *can* be counted on to encourage those qualities that ensure the continued evolution of life on our planet. If what you want to do in life builds character, instills faith, allows for acceptance, creates more love, and if this is in keeping with the resolution of your issue, then chances are the universe will support you in obtaining the answer you seek—or something even greater than you've yet imagined. The odds will be with you because your drive to resolve your problem is, in truth, the unseen order manifesting through you. Tao, life force, the universe, God—however you choose to refer to the unseen powers—operate only in support of your awakening to your full spiritual potential as a life-driven human being. Your real responsibility is to let go of your illusions of control and to trust in your intuitive spirit. Trust that which inspires you. Allow yourself to be a vehicle for the unseen powers, and allow your problems to resolve as the by-product of this commitment.

✸ Process: *Eleven Questions*

You are going to be presented with eleven questions. Take as long as you want or need on each. Five minutes per question should be more than adequate.

Unlike past writing assignments, this time you are invited to engage with your left-brain as fully and completely as you wish. Don't worry, in fact, about whether the voice that is responding is left or right brain, instead think only of bringing the very best you are capable of at the moment to this process, trusting that the most appropriate balances and most evolved voices will be working with you toward the resolution you seek. (Of course, you can always submit your conclusions to the board of director's process established in the previous hour, if you so choose.)

Question Number One:

What issue would you most like to resolve right now?

This may be the issue that you have been working with all day, but don't be surprised if suddenly something brand-new and unexpected comes up for you. There's no need to struggle to get exactly the right issue. Whatever occurs to you now will be perfect. It is important to take your issues one by one as they arise. You can always come back and do this process again, focusing on your original problem, if—as is so often the case—it hasn't already been resolved as a by-product of doing the work on the issue that has come up for you at this time.

Question Number Two:

What outcome would you most like to achieve?

Finally, here is your opportunity to ask for what you really want. You don't need to be rational or practical—or surrendered and accepting. At this stage, it is important to be willing to tell the truth about your desires and needs. Whether your goals are achievable or not should not be taken into consideration.

Can you give yourself this much permission to dream? Your yearning is sacred space. Honor and respect your heart's desire, even if it brings in its wake irresolution and restlessness, doubt or fear. The truth of what you want is the very stuff of life.

Set your ambition as a directional pointer, a lodestar to help your spirit finds its way. While it is true that you have been previously asked to surrender the stress and drive connected with the setting of goals, you must still set goals. There is nothing wrong with envisioning and going after your dreams. You have the right to your desires and yearnings. You have the right to ask for what you truly want. You have the right to a relationship with the unseen order that makes sense of your life. Just remember to leave room for the miracle that you may not get what you asked for: you may get something even greater than expected. Don't let your goals limit the possibilities.

Question Number Three:

How have you tried to resolve this situation so far?

What if you were to see your efforts, regardless of the results, as the acts of a hero—rather than a victim? You know about heroes. Think about a Saturday afternoon action film—Jason or Ulysses. Monstrous Claymation figures rearing up their heads, fire flashing between their teeth, swords slashing at rubber skin. Now let me ask you something. When is it that you think of Jason as a hero? Only in the last moment, when the monster lies panting on the ground, or the fleece is secured safely in hand? Of course not. Jason is a hero from the time the first titles come up on the screen. When the monster momentarily has the upper hand, Jason is still the hero. Why? Because you have faith that he, in the end, will prevail.

Now let me ask you another question. When do you get to be a hero in your life? Only on the day when you finally get your first BMW? At the meeting with your boss when the promotion comes in as hoped for? When the letter arrives accepting your son at his number one college? But how about when the BMW breaks down, you hate the new job, your child drops out of school to "find himself"? At these moments, can you extend to yourself the same concept of heroism you extend to the classic movie stars you pay good money to see? How about honoring yourself not only when you are standing on the mountain with golden fleece raised high, but also when you are willing to engage with all the Medusas and dragons that pop up in your life?

Question Number Four:

What was it about this approach that did not work?

Your greatest mistake has given you the greatest gift: the elimination of one option you will never have to do again. William James writes:

> The individual, so far as he suffers from his wrongness and criticizes it, is to that extent consciously beyond it, and in at least possible touch with something higher. . . . He becomes conscious that this higher part is conterminous and continuous with a MORE of the same quality, which is operative in the universe outside of him, and which he can keep in working touch with, and in a fashion get on board of and save himself when all his lower being has gone to pieces in the wreck.

Question Number Five:

What payoff or benefit have you received from having this situation in your life?

There is always some payoff, hard as it may be for you to admit it right now. Have you received attention for this problem? Compassion? Has this problem taken you places, into therapy or workshops, bought presents for you, such as this book? What good has come to you because of the issue you have chosen to deal with today?

Question Number Six:

What other way could you get the same payoff that would be better for you?

All this time, you have been quietly growing stronger. You have patiently waited for the moment to arrive for you to come forward and claim a better way for yourself, to demand your rightful respect and dignity. Until today, perhaps you thought that this moment of reclamation could come only when you perfected yourself: you have worked so hard for self-mastery, trying to be good enough to silence those voices that would exploit and undermine you. *The I Ching* teaches:

> It is only when we have the courage to face things exactly as they are, without any sort of self-deception or illusion, that a light will develop out of events, by which the path to success may be recognized.

Question Number Seven:

What can you change about this situation?

This is a question that will require honesty and courage. You will have to sort through the jumbled threads that complicate many of the issues you face, figuring out which you can do something about and which you can't. Perhaps this seems hopeless. But there is always something you can change about the issue you face. If you can't change the circumstances, you can change your attitude about the situation. At this point in the process, perhaps it is too much to ask yourself what can be done to resolve your issue. But in any case, you can easily ask yourself what it is you can do that will contribute to creating the optimum conditions within which to find the resolution you seek.

Question Number Eight:

What must you accept about this situation?

You can influence your external world—but you can't force it to do your bidding. When the escape route of your illusions has been cut off, you are forced to deal with the issue of who *you* are—devoid of false hope, and other people's opinions. You ask yourself: What is achievable now that the fantasies have been stripped away? Release your illusions, and there may be a moment when it feels as if the very construction of your life is about to disassemble. Let it go. Trust that it will be preferable to have the humblest structure of a life built on solid ground—than the most elaborate one, built on sand. When you can admit how much of your foundation has been built on the unstable ground of illusion, you find that you are free to take more risks in your life. Why? Because you realize that all along, you had less to lose than you'd feared.

Question Number Nine:

What is your greatest fear about this situation?

The nature of risk-taking, at its core, is fear of the unknown. Usually, we're afraid of what we can't control because we are, in truth, afraid of failure. This fear of failure is what got us into the "old paradigm" control model in the first place. This does not mean that you will never feel fear. It is normal, human, and often quite appropriate to feel anxiety about taking a risk.

It is imperative, especially when you are in transition, to let yourself feel all of your emotions: sadness and grief over what is passing; inspiration about new possibilities; and sweet anticipation as you recognize and make room for the exciting new ways of being that are taking root in your soul. You are using a wider band of your human potential. You are more firmly grounded in what is real, less likely to have fallen asleep at the wheel of life's illusions.

The question, in fact, is not how to stop being afraid. Rather, the issue is how can you include your fear as a normal and healthy part of the broad spectrum of feelings that makes us more fully human?

Question Number Ten:

What is the truth about this situation?

When you tell the truth, make sure you tell the whole truth. Are you one of those people who wallows in the drama of your life, thrashing about in the underbelly of your emotions? When you tell the whole truth, you must be willing to acknowledge and accept what is positive about you and your situation as well as those aspects you wish you could change. It is sometimes tempting to dissolve in a morass of self-pity disguised as self-improvement. But tell the whole truth and you will realize that while some things may be falling apart, other things are, at the same time, falling together.

Question Number Eleven:

What one thing are you now willing to do to get the resolution you seek?

When the passion of your inner imperative grows stronger than your fears, you have access to a self that is fully available to receive the level of resolution you truly desire and deserve. The individual who began this process is not the same person who has now arrived at question number eleven. Sometimes the thing you must be willing to do requires you to take some action in the world—sometimes the action you need to take will be within the confines of your own heart. You may not know for sure what the outcome of your action will be. There are no guarantees. But one thing is certain. When you begin to act, you set forces in motion that will ultimately bring you into alignment with the unseen order. Trust that you are in exactly the right place at the right time for the fullest realization of your greatest good for all concerned.

Eleven Sample Questions

Question Number One:

What issue would you most like to resolve right now?

I'm angry and upset that I'm not being considered for the new management position that opened up at my company. I'm the most qualified person for the position and I don't know why they aren't considering me.

Question Number Two:

What outcome would you most like to achieve?

I want that position.

Question Number Three:

How have you tried to resolve this situation so far?

I've tried to do brilliant work they would notice so that they would think of me for the job.

Question Number Four:

What was it about this approach that did not work?

I quite simply don't think they thought of me—or maybe they think I don't want it.

Question Number Five:

What payoff or benefit have you received from having this situation in your life?

I didn't realize how much I want that position.

Question Number Six:

What other way could you get the same payoff that would be better for you?

I could take more time to think about my career and strategize about what I really want and how to get it, instead of working all the time. I guess it's been kind of a safe way to hang out, not saying anything. That way I don't have to take the risk of being turned down.

Question Number Seven:

What can you change about this situation?

I haven't let my boss know that I want the job and that I think I can do it. I can change not being considered to being considered. This seems awfully scary to me. What if he turns me down?

Question Number Eight:

What must you accept about this situation?

If I take the risk, it doesn't mean he will give me the job. I have to accept that all I can do is all I can do—that I can't control what he does. Right now, I'm feeling too nervous about the whole thing. I need to accept that I'm not up to taking the risk.

Question Number Nine:

What is your greatest fear about this situation?

That I'll get fired.

Question Number Ten:

What is the truth about this situation?

That they would never fire me over suggesting myself for the position. I have done a great job, and it is possible that they think I don't want the promotion.

Question Number Eleven:

What one thing are you now willing to do to get the resolution you seek?

It's too scary to think about going to the boss—but I could go to his assistant and see if they had been considering me for the job. I don't want to feel like an idiot, but it's more important to me than I thought. I'll ask his assistant for the inside scoop—and then decide whether to proceed or not. Tomorrow morning, first thing, I'll go see his assistant. I know now how much I want this job. In fact, if it turns out that I handled this as badly as I think I have and the opportunity is blown, I'm going to sign up for a session with that career counselor my friend Paul keeps telling me about, to get some advice about what to do next.

Fifteen

What's A Dream Worth?

There are at least two among you, I am sure, who would lay at my feet your toughest problem—the one that there's no way to solve by sunset.

The first of you asks: How about one having to do with money? There's nothing more real than money, you say.

It is getting toward dark now, and you are crying out to me that you're burned out. You are desperate to make changes in your life —to take risks. It's just that you don't have the monetary/physical/emotional resources to resolve your issue. You're trapped!

To you who claim a willingness of the spirit but a disobedience of the pocketbook I ask: What if you suddenly had $60,000 and several years to use as you pleased? What would you do with that time and that money? Would it be enough to get you unstuck and into a new place, perhaps closer to where your heart has been urging you to go? What would you do? Would you start your own consulting group? Go back to school to learn new skills? Do an internship to pave the way toward a new career? Search full time for a better job? Relocate to another part of the world where you can live for a fraction of the cost?

These are not just fanciful musings, since I'm now smack dab in the middle of a school full of individuals who somehow carved the time and money out of their lives to prepare for something new, a student's life at Divinity School. Here are people of all ages who have been called upon to answer the question "Just what are my dreams worth?" They have scraped together a combination of loans, personal savings, mortgaged homes, part-time jobs, and scholarships, many of which will have to be repaid once they graduate. This much is true: you're not likely find a poorer, more vital, or inspired group.

Of course, you would prefer not to use your life savings/compromise your lifestyle/go into debt/take risks concerning the future. But you have to ask yourself the simple, telling question: *What are my dreams worth?* Are you willing to put your comfort and security on the line in order to underwrite your transition? True, there is more recognition and support for school loans and the modest life of a student than there may be for the sacrifice it would take to pursue your dreams. But why shouldn't anyone in the corporate or professional world wanting to make a major life transition give themselves the same level of faith in their future as my fellow students have in theirs?

Here's my suggestion. First of all, fantasize about what it would cost and how much time it would take to bring you closer to living your dream. Then, brainstorm sources of funding. Develop a repayment schedule that begins when your transition is complete and your new income source is producing for you.

But there's risk involved with this, you say. Ah hah! You've put your finger right on the button. You thought your inability to resolve your issue by sunset was a money and resource problem. It is not. It is a faith problem.

You see, we have misunderstood faith profoundly over the past several decades. How many times—from how many self-help books, talk-show guests, and celebrity gurus—have you heard that "if you follow your heart, your dreams will come true"? This is considered to be "faith." Even James Redfield's *The Celestine Prophecy,* while teaching about surrender and acceptance, posits the notion that if you bring yourself into alignment with the universal energy flow, your vegetables will grow bigger than the next guy's. How easy it is to slip from trusting in the unseen order that acts through us—regardless of how the results may appear to ourselves or others at any given moment—into the more mechanistic, utilitarian deal we try to cut with the divine, which is if we do our bit to get into align-ment, we will get a winning hand. The truth is that faith is not about what God can do for us. Many of us (myself included) spend time communing with our inner wisdom, letting go of illusions, taking courageous spiritual risks, opening ourselves to messages from others and the environment, and feeling our pain. Does this entitle us to stand with outstretched arms to receive our just rewards? As if we could be spiritual enough to get our lives to turn out for us just the way we think we want? And yet, when I hear people talking about "creating your own reality," I have a hunch this is exactly what they mean. One of my favorite stories illustrates this point.

It was with arms thus outstretched that my friend Denise came to understand how easy it is to go awry in the spiritual process even with the best intentions. Denise was at a point in her life where she was confused about whether to stay in the catering business she had operated for twenty years with her husband, Joe, or to follow her heart into the unknown and embark full-time on her private ambi-tion to write cookbooks. Joe was enthusiastic about the possibilities that were opening up for Denise—but leaving the catering business meant that Denise would be relying on Joe to carry the full responsibility for their income for some time. Deeply conflicted about her possible defection, Denise went on a personal retreat to the woods, promising to be absolutely courageous, honest, and diligent in her efforts to be spiritual. As a result, she spent much of the day struggling to quell her left-brain rational processes and let intuitive knowing flood over her. She could feel the resolution to her issues eager to burst through into consciousness. At a fever pitch of anticipation, everything she encountered seemed meaningful. She felt she was on the verge of a breakthrough, but then she began to itch. She had inadvertently selected the special spot for her retreat in the middle of a thick, green patch of poison ivy.

As the acute itching spread over her body, she turned her complaints to God.

"God," she asked, "what did I do wrong? I'm trying to do what's right. I'm bringing everything I've got to this process. Why did I do this? What could possibly be the lesson in this?"

The answer came to her kindly but firmly.

"You humans. Your notion of your place in the universe is so grandiose. There was a lesson here indeed. But not for you. This one was for the ivy."

Try as we might to ensure that our goals are met, there is this quirky thing that we positive-thinking people hate to take into consideration: fate. Whatever you choose to call it—destiny, accident, life lesson, karma—fate is more likely than not to spin your life out of your control from time to time. Native American, African, and Aboriginal cultures knew enough about this to have named the presence of "trickster" gods, whose purpose it is to use mischief as a means of awakening and guiding humanity to enlightenment.

So, if you can't act in such a way as to ensure that you will get what you want—and if you can't *not* act on your own behalf, what are you supposed to do? Surrender does not mean that you let these unpredictable forces have their way with you. Surrender is not the same as resignation. Surrender is simply this: to do what you must.

As Denise was recovering from the poison ivy, she finally got the resolution she'd been hoping for. Having shorted out her lesson-seeking circuitry, she caught herself in the act of living her life. She recognized that she had already been shutting down her ambitions concerning catering and opening up the possibilities of writing her cookbook for some time. She'd made her decision. She caught the reality of this transition in the popular song lyrics that hummed in the background of her consciousness; it was in the absent-minded mistakes she'd begun to make for the first time in her catering career —and the amount of time she spent before her computer screen; it had been pressing forward through her unremembered daydreams and her disregarded hopes. When she finally caught herself in the act of becoming a full-time writer of cookbooks, it was the most natural thing in the world. When she released her grip on "reality," she allowed the circumstances of her life to reconfigure around who, in truth, she had already become.

Why hadn't she realized that she'd made her decision sooner? Because she knew that there was risk involved. It was a risk she had always believed herself willing to take—as soon as she knew for sure it would work out for her in the end. But the irony is that if you know for sure it's not going to cost you anything, it's not truly a risk. If you are courageous enough to tune in to the yearnings of your heart, you will discover a taskmaster far more demanding than any of the external forces you ever allowed to call the shots in your life. You are right to hesitate before you cross the threshhold in order to consider the seriousness of the commitment of what it means to be fully alive.

Ask yourself: If I take the risk and the worst happens, am I prepared to deal with the circumstances and the emotions that might result? (It's also useful, by the way, to ask yourself what the best possible result could be. In my experience, the odds are that fate will put your own results somewhere in the middle. Most people don't get everything they ask for every time, but neither do they get nothing.)

If the worst does happen, though, could you live with it? Is the risk worth it? If not, consider a less extreme approach that will cut the potential negative consequences to a load you would be willing to bear. There's a simple way to tell if you've made the right decision: pick too big a goal, and you will feel overwhelmed. Pick too small a goal, and you'll be bored. Pick something between the two extremes and you will end up on what in Eastern philosophy, is called "the Middle Road." Once you have properly defined your boundaries, give your goals everything you've got and understand that "everything" includes taking the time to care for your physical, emotional, and spiritual needs along the way. You must be willing to honor your human limitations and pay respect to a mischievous universe that might have a surprise or two up its sleeve. The key to having the experience of success you seek in your life is to come to recognize those challenges that are worthy of you, with consequences that you are willing to bear.

Another person who was willing to take such a risk was Larry, a friend from New York. All of Larry's life, he dreamed of making money with his art. Meanwhile, he paid the bills by doing accounting work. For twenty-five years, his life had been split in two. By day, he wore a business suit and engaged in the world of commerce. At night and on weekends, he threw on old jeans, grabbed his watercolors, and explored both his inner and outer worlds in paint.

"Wouldn't it be great to be able to paint day and night?" he thought. Excited by the prospect, he mortgaged his home to finance a major life transition. He would simplify his lifestyle and use the money to open a studio/gallery where he could paint full-time and sell his work. Caught up in the excitement, he quit his job, found and renovated warehouse space in an up-and-coming part of town, and at long last set out to make his life's passion his life's work. He had given himself a year to make it work. He was following his bliss, so surely his money would soon arrive.

When his studio was finally ready for occupancy, Larry eagerly took up his brushes, positioned himself before the blank canvas, and froze. He realized to his chagrin that he couldn't think of a thing to paint. After twenty-five years of nonstop creativity, artist's block set in! He walked from easel to coffeepot to bed listlessly, wondering why the well had run dry. As days dragged into weeks, and weeks into months, Larry thought about the role of art in his life—what "doing what you love" really meant to him.

He soon understood that before he decided to try to make money at it, painting was the one place where he could be totally free. It was his version of journal writing, a place of self-expression and spontaneous creativity that helped him make sense of his life. That other people liked his art or had opinions about it had always been incidental. In his heart, he didn't at all want to deal with the reality of whether or not people cared about his work, let alone their being willing to pay for it.

When the reality of having to make money off his art sank in, he was forced to confront the fact that the vast majority of professional artists were able to make compromises that he was simply unwilling to make. He understood this the first day he opened his doors and the crowds that he had imagined failed to materialize. It dawned on him that if he were to succeed, he could not spend his days painting as he'd imagined. Rather, he'd have to spend large chunks of time marketing his art, networking with patrons, talking with them about their living rooms' color schemes, and so on. So what did Larry do?

After a great deal of soul-searching, he realized that he was unwilling to turn his paintings into a commodity. But having made the investment in an art gallery, he would use his business skills to make a go of it—selling other people's art. This move brought him into the world of art, where he yearned to be, much better than working as a corporate accountant. If he couldn't be the one artist in 100,000 whose uncompromised work created sufficient demand to support his lifestyle, at least he could make his peace with life's limitations while wearing his paint-spattered jeans. Meanwhile, the internal drive to create returned and his art once again flourished—after business hours.

Several years after all of this transpired, I bumped into Larry, who was glowing with excitement. Apparently, a short time after the gallery had been successfully launched, Larry had hung a few of his own paintings in stray corners. After two years, he had just sold his first piece to someone other than family or friends, for $75. Larry was a very happy man.

Watch out for that part of you that wants to anticipate every negative possibility. Of course you would like to take a stand and then have everything turn out just the way you want. But life will break loose from your grip from time to time. Can you find the courage to do what is in your heart to do—and be willing to take the consequences? This will be easier for you to do if you realize that while you are only human, and therefore obligated to surrender to the fact that you can't control all the bad things that happen to you, it is also true that you can't control the good things that happen to you, either. When you surrender the illusion of your control over external reality, you not only admit to your helplessness to prevent problems from occurring, but you must, in truth, admit that you cannot prevent solutions from coming, either.

When you are willing to do what's next, there are never any dead ends. What may seem to be a failure, like Larry's artist's block, may well be a stepping-stone to an end even more fulfilling than you'd anticipated. You are not in the position to judge your outcomes. As long as you are alive, you are in the middle of your story. You don't know what the ending will be. It is entirely possible that the time-table that is truly best for the growth of your character and your spirit may not be the same timetable that your ego prefers. Reaffirm your willingness to handle whatever comes up, trusting that the same process that got you through this far will see you through to the other side—perhaps even during the next and final hour before sunset.

There's another possibility to consider at this juncture. What if you have already gotten your answer and just didn't know it? Maybe your selective perception, impatience, or plain tendency toward fantasy got in the way of recognizing the truth. When you're at the exact point where real transformation is possible, you have the opportunity, yet again, to consider whether you really believe that the universe is supportive of your growth. What is called for is not to create your reality, but to take a leap of faith into a realm beyond your control. This is asking a lot of you, I know. But on the other hand, just exactly how much is your dream worth to you?

Sixteen

A Problem Worthy of You

I began the previous chapter by suggesting that there are at least two among you who would lay your toughest problem at my feet: the issue that cannot possibly be solved by sunset. Just now, I addressed the first among you, the one whose persistent problem was not so much due to a lack of resources, luck, or opportunity as it was to a lack of faith. I believe in you and I trust that you may yet have your breakthrough by sunset this very evening.

But there is another, the second among you, who has challenged me to help you resolve your toughest problem. You know exactly who you are. For you are one for whom much of the material covered in this book is familiar ground—and still your issue persists.

You are someone who has allowed yourself to participate in the wider range of the human potential, not content with indulging in superficial distractions in an effort to explore only the brighter spectrum of emotions—welcome feelings, like happiness, contentment, and joy. But you whose yearning has become so great, it has broken open your heart. For it is you who feel for others' suffering, for wasted potential, for a world too often under seige by greed, ignorance, and evil. You have followed your emotions and spirit into the more richly leavened territory of empathy and compassion. You have allowed yourself to love deeply, hope foolishly, and grieve wholly. Even though you may wish for resolution, you intuit that the problem you have brought to the table today does not belong to you alone. It belongs to our entire generation—and to all time. I can understand why you seek relief from the pain of being fully alive, but I cannot promise you relief. It is too important for our society to have someone such as you—someone who has come to stand for something larger than one's self, and who is willing to take the consequences.

But even to you I hold out the possibility of resolution. This will come to you effortlessly, naturally, when your spirit has grown big enough to encompass everything. Resist the urge to rush for answers as a way to come to a superficial resolution. You are strong enough to embrace it all.

Shortly after Dan and I made the decision to cut our hours back and reclaim a healthier relationship to success in our lives, a number of clients—and employees—jumped off what they perceived to be a sinking ship. They did not understand that by putting our own needs and desires back into the equation, and allowing the company and our lives to reconfigure around this new, higher center, we were engaging in a heroic act that would eventually benefit us all.

Recently, rummaging for my daughter's sleeping bag, I stumbled across my journal from that period in my life. Mixed in with temper tantrums, reports of babies needing diapers changed, and flooded basements, were the seeds of the philosophy that continue to bear fruit in my life, reminding me that it is in the mud where new growth is most likely to take root. Just after my thirty-seventh birthday, at the moment when it looked for all the world like our business had fallen apart, I came home to write in my journal:

> Ghosts—presences of what and who I used to be, the employees and clients I once surrounded myself with—stalk our half-empty offices. Big enough for 30, 5 of us rattle around. Something is crashing, dying. I feel it is for the good—but I have no answers. No easy solutions, only Dan's arms around me, Jody and Grant loving me. My loving them, in a way I never thought possible. The sweet support of the few staff who remain. A kaleidoscope of pain and change—to what? I want to get out lists and numbers and calculators and organize reality into something that will work. But that is for later—much later. This is the time for me to let go—to be simple. To meditate, to write. To love and be loved. I have skills that I bring to serve clients. I trust there is a need for what we do. That much I know. But who should I hire? Can we afford more staff? How big should we be? NO! I cry out. Enough! Enough linear thinking. Enough needing to know what to do.
>
> What a stretch for me—to function responsibly, not having to know the answer. To let go, and watch myself evolve. Surrender. I can start by doing what my soul beckons me to do. Do I resign the client who has not yet let us go but who is making unreasonable demands, even though we need the income? Is that irresponsible? I keep trying to force an answer, instead of flowing with each moment. This is a beautiful moment right now: so sad, so full. I am fighting to be free and it hurts . . . afraid that every passing moment is an opportunity for my life to unravel even more. Where's the bottom? At least I know I will be alive to witness it when it has been reached.

Among the employees who left were several who had unpleasant things to say about our transformation. I would like to report that they went on to have bad experiences with their future employment situations and having subsequently come to see the light, recognized publicly the superiority of our approach. But the truth is that several of them formed an agency competitive with ours, taking with them some of our clients. At last report, running their company along old paradigm lines, they were doing well and were totally unrepentent. As terrible as it feels when bad things happen to good people, it is almost worst when it appears that good things are happening for "bad" people. If this is truly an orderly and loving universe, how could this possibly be justified? In the Western religion model, we are comforted by the idea of judgment for them—and an eternity in hell. In the East Indian tradition, we encounter karma, the idea that they will pay for their bad deeds in their next life. In Confucian philosophy, "inferior people" are shown to be like swamp plants, growing huge and glorious overnight, but gone by the next day, while goodness, like a tiny acorn, grows slowly and steadily, sending its roots in deep and prevailing in the end. But my favorite explanation, based on samurai legend, came to me from my karate sensei.

A samurai went to see a spiritual master.

"Show me the door to heaven and the door to hell," he demanded.

"You stupid samurai. I can't show this to somebody as dumb as you." With that, the samurai pulled out his sword and threatened to kill the master.

"That is the door to hell," the sensei patiently explained. Becoming enlightened, the samurai put away his sword.

"And that is the door to heaven."

✳

Despite the painful defections, in short order the Orsborn Group Public Relations grew back to its previous gross revenue, close to the half-million dollar mark, with that same loyal core who had remained doing the work that had taken nearly twenty to do previously. When we had the courage to do things like resign from the hotel client that was making unreasonable demands of us during the Gulf War, we had our vitality returned to us. When we were fired by Embarcadero Center, we didn't burn ourselves out with useless resistance or self-flagellation. We had our vital energy available to us to create a new future, rather than to continue to react to our rapidly —albeit painfully—receding past.

We were freed of abusive clients and counterproductive employees. What we were left with was a team of explorers who together discovered the joys and efficiencies of committed teamwork. There was no time wasted complaining about each other at the water cooler, no meetings about meetings because we were afraid to take responsibility for an action, to take a risk. We were creative, alive, excited, on fire. The bottom line was that with our overhead greatly reduced, our profits soared. And we accomplished this with forty-hour-or-less weeks, with time for outside hobbies, relationships, commitments, service to others and to our own richly enhanced lives.

Our success was the by-product of the growth and spirit of our relationships and of ourselves as individuals. As painful as the process was, it was worth the struggle.

I have found, even during moments as challenging as the one I just shared with you, resolution beyond what I would have thought possible. The resolution I have found—and that is possible for you, regardless of the situation you are facing in your life—is a sense of bittersweet acceptance, a quiet, melancholy knowing that infuses all of life with meaning. I experience the emotional color of spirituality as free-floating longing for fulfillment. It is a yearning that I have come to value even more than what I used to call "happiness." For when my primary purpose was to be happy, I invested much of my vital energy in protecting myself from the threat of discomfort or upset. I limited my intimate relationships, knowing they contained the potential for pain. I worked hard to obtain things that would increase my comfort—a better house, a bigger client, a nicer car. But since it was these things that brought me happiness, my happiness was dependent on forces from outside myself. What came to me from outside myself could also be taken away. I lived in a constant state of anxiety.

Only when my love of life and faith in the future grew greater than my fear of pain, could I find a state of resolution that could be depended upon, regardless of the problems I faced at any given time. I have discovered an amazing thing: You can't depend on the circumstances of your life to bring you the fulfillment you seek. The experience of fulfillment must come first. This is a resolution that can not be forced or faked.

It has been a challenge for you, as someone who has sought true resolution all these years, because you are already too wise and too honest to sweep away what others can ignore, explain, or simply avoid. Perhaps you wondered if there weren't some better answer—something you could do, have, or be—to have it turn out easier, simpler for you, for those you care about, and for the world. By the end of this chapter, you will know for sure if there's something more you can do. If you are already doing enough, you can now have resolution by being who you already are in the company of others who share your yearning.

We, who feel the pain, are the truth-tellers. The generation whose legacy has been Auschwitz, the atom bomb, the deaths of Martin Luther King Jr. and John Fitzgerald Kennedy, Vietnam, and the tragedy in Oklahoma. We face a world in crisis politically, environmentally, socially, and spiritually. In a world so out of synch, it is perhaps among the most unsettled and troubled of us that we find the most vital spirits. We have learned over the years that money and external success alone—while they can often give a pretty good imitation of short-term fulfillment—cannot truly protect you from the pain of living. More recently, we have been mastering an even harder lesson: that our spiritual efforts to make deals with God to give us what we want are doomed to fall short as well.

Through our spiritual lives we may be comforted, we may gain insight and wisdom, we may receive an innate sense of morality, we may obtain faith in the hope of ultimate goodness and order prevailing. But we must also confront the fact that all of us share a creation that can allow nature, human and otherwise, to be at times capricious and cruel. There is suffering. There is pain. There is evil. And to look to the development of our spiritual lives solely as a source of comfort or protection, or of power and control—using faith as armor against the pain and doubt that an honest engagement with a living universe demands of us—is dangerous.

What do I mean by dangerous? As a Jewish woman born the same year as the state of Israel, who lost relatives in the Holocaust whom I never had the opportunity to meet, I feel every day and every moment how important it is for each of us to keep at the forefront of our consciousness not only our goodness and our morality but our darker potentialities. It was well-meaning people, after all, people who didn't want to make trouble, who wanted to live as happy a life as possible under the circumstances, who attended church and participated in their children's sports and lessons, who were the architects who designed the shower facilities, the book-keepers who paid the bills for the cyanide.

We each contain the potential to ignore, legitimize, or suppress our darker impulses in order to proceed with "business as usual." Ironically, when you are unwilling to face the uncomfortable truth about yourself and the universe, you give your moral discomfort away to others who would offer you solace and superficial solutions in its place. Equally dangerous is the attempt to rely solely on left-brain rationality, denying yourself access to a working knowledge of your intuitive, creative, and spiritual potential. By default, you allow your unconsciously held impulses to call the shots. Those of you who have envisioned your relationship to spirituality as a way of avoiding or minimizing discomfort should consider the possibility that the demands of true faith will inevitably lead to struggle. You will struggle through your arrogance to discover humility; you will struggle through your glibness to find your deeper yearnings; you will struggle through your rationalizations and avoidances to confront the mystery of a divine power that allows catastrophes; you will struggle through your illusions of comfort and control to feel your own pain as well as the pain of others.

In the trenches, wrestling as Jacob did at the Jabbok River, you are called both to struggle with God and with your own humanity. You must surrender to the possibility that we are all at a moment of baby steps, not giant leaps, as our generation's legacy forces our understanding of what is truly being asked of us to go deeper and yet deeper.

Those who feel called to serve humanity in these troubled times must be willing to take it all on. Rabbi Irving Greenberg wrote, in his book *Cloud of Smoke, Pillar of Fire:*

> After Auschwitz, faith means that there are times when faith is overcome . . . We now have to speak of "moment faiths" . . . interspersed with times when the flames and smoke of the burning children blot out faith, although it flickers again . . . The difference between the skeptic and the believer is frequency of faith, and not certitude of position.

Against this backdrop, and pitted against these odds, is there nothing you can do to ensure the resolution of issues that may not only require the best efforts of our generation—but of generations to come?

We cry out for inner peace, but perhaps it is time for us to confront the darker truth that spiritual maturity may march us, often against our wills, to the brink of righteous anger, tempered with forgiveness. We must, when moved by the spirit of our souls, be willing to take a stand. My favorite author of fiction, Pearl Buck, speaks directly to you in her *Voice in the House:*

> Against the tyranny of the inferior man, the superior man also has the right to be free. . . . For good people to feel pain and to take action against the inferior is the hope of humanity.

You must be willing to honor yourself for your willingness to engage in the struggle—regardless of the results. You must confront the fact that you may not be able to save the world single-handedly, while you remain willing to add your two cents' worth of common sense and moral decency whenever you can.

As my good friend Donna Paz can be counted on to remind me when I express my frustration with my failed schemes to change the world, there is, at least, always the potential to achieve a "smaller good." You may not have a meaningful career that allows you to make the kind of contribution you feel the urge to make, but you can take a job where you can make a living while protecting and preserving enough of your vitality to engage positively with and through other aspects of your life. You may find a problem worthy of you—one that is worth the investment of a lifetime, and beyond. Whatever the outcome, you can offer bittersweet acceptance to yourself and the world knowing that your best shot will come from being more of who and what you are at any given moment. This includes joy as well as despair; moments of genius as well as moments of failure; clarity as well as confusion. Surrendering to this—being able and willing to embrace it all at the same time—is where you will find the resolution you seek.

How does one's spirit grow large enough to encompass everything?

Joseph Campbell offers this advice: "When the world seems to be falling apart, stick to your own trajectory; hang on to your own ideals and find kindred spirits. That's the rule of life."

You can begin by engaging fully with your life at whatever level your life presents itself to you. If your life is a mess, then engage with the mess. If you find yourself too fascinated by how horrible you are, break the negative feedback loop by taking the focus off yourself and think about doing something for somebody else.

In that same recently rediscovered, journal, was an invocation I'd written called "My Ordinary Self Is Enough."

My ordinary self is enough.
When I express my ordinary feelings, I impact others.
When I feel inadequate, I can ask for help.
When I'm afraid, I can be vulnerable.
When I make mistakes, I can correct and move on.
I can do what needs to be done feeling relaxed and unpressured.
When I am my ordinary self, my attention is off of me and on others.
I can listen.
I can care.
I am enough, regardless of the opportunities I have or may miss.
My ordinary self is enough.

On September 30, 1987, after a particularly painful spell of feeling sorry for myself, I had a rare and precious experience of what ordinariness feels like.

I woke up yesterday, feeling like dust. My writing was dust. My ambition to change the world was dust. My wisdom was dust. As I was dust, I watched my life bump along with all the daily catastrophes that normally take me under. Since I was already basically nowhere, I brought no resistance to things. When the car started to smoke, Dan and I merely put it in neutral and drifted into a gas station. Giving up our plans to go into San Francisco for dinner, we took the opportunity to explore the gas station's neighborhood while we waited for the car to be fixed. In this way, we stumbled onto what turned out to be the best pizza place in Marin.

Anyway, I woke up this morning bursting with love for no particular reason. I think of moments: Dan crossing the finish line of the Dipsea Race, sweat dripping off his salt and pepper hair. Grant playing his first piece of real music on the piano for grandma and grandpa. Mom and I holding hands. Jody nestled in my lap. All the while I felt cautious at the happiness, praising God while simultaneously worrying that I would somehow become enmeshed in the kind of reward and punishment thinking that gets me into trouble. Then I remembered the advice of a friend.

She said, "When good things happen, take them to be the universe acknowledging you for how wonderful you are. When bad things happen, take them as unlucky accidents that have nothing to do with who you are or what you've done."

And so it is that I have finally figured out the secret to life: When I have love in my heart, things go the best they can. If they don't, when engulfed by love, who cares?

The Jewish writer A. J. Heschel tells the story of a Hasidic teacher who sat down to study a volume of the Talmud. A day later, his students noticed that he had not moved off the first page. Guessing that he was puzzling over a particularly difficult passage, they let him be. But when several more days passed, noting that the rebbe was still on that same page, they spoke up to inquire as to why he had not gone on with his studies.

"But," replied the rebbe, "I feel so good here. Why should I go elsewhere?"

When one of the emperors of China asked the Zen master Bidhidharma what enlightenment was, his answer was "Lots of space, nothing holy."

Your ordinary self is enough. Resolution will come when you let go of your illusions—particularly the one that tells you how spiritual you are, how great your contributions will be. You let go even of this.

Let go of your left-brain reactions: making things happen, trying, working, figuring things out, efforting, preserving, protecting; controlling. You do this by relaxing. Let your right brain have its moment, finding a way to grow through the concrete of your busy thoughts and actions. When you find this balance, you will become absolutely ordinary. You will not need to try hard to fit into the unseen order of the universe. You already do.

HOUR
NUMBER
SEVEN
UNTIL
SUNSET

Ready
to
Receive

Seventeen

A Ritual of Completion

*One day in retrospect the years of struggle will strike you as
the most beautiful.*
—*Sigmund Freud*

Throughout the day, you have been giving yourself the opportunity to resolve your problem, exploring new ways of interacting with your issues and your problem-solving process overall. It is hoped you are feeling enriched by the things you have been learning about yourself along the way.

These are assets that will assist you in making better decisions about the problems and issues you face, not only today but for all of your life. This is vital since your life consists of all the decisions you have made along the way: who the people in your life are and how you relate to them; your work; your commitments; your health; your spiritual, moral, and emotional challenges. The quality of these decisions depends on the quality of information you have available to you. Today's exploration of right-brain experiences has provided you with an expanded range of possibilities and new resources upon which to call when faced with problems and issues that have resisted the kind of left-brain processes relied upon in the past.

However you feel about the problem or issue you initially brought into this day for resolution, it is important to note that none of today's growth would have happened if you hadn't had this particular problem to deal with at this time.

This is a good opportunity to take a moment to pause and reflect on the progress you've made toward resolution, and your current feelings about the problem or issue that brought you to this day's engagement. You are about to begin the first of a four-part process that will constitute the heart of this final hour's important work—the task of completion.

✸ Process: *Completion*

At this time, I'd like you to begin by reading through your writing in response to the first hour's process of the day, "Setting Your Intention." Doesn't it seem like you wrote that exercise a long time ago? How do you feel about the person who wrote that document? Do you feel at this point you have some of the answers you were searching for? Have you accomplished some/all of what you intended? What do you now know that you didn't know then? Take some time to reflect on the gifts this day has brought you—as well as any questions and yearnings that remain unanswered. After you have done this, take a few minutes to review the entire day. Reread all of your writings from the previous processes, remember your experiences, check in on how you felt about your problem, yourself, and this process then, and how you feel about them now. When you have done so, return to this page and we will continue on together.

✸

Earlier in this book, I spoke about how people who are fully alive are free to appreciate the fuller range of possibilities that life offers: despair and joy, failure and success, will and surrender, death and rebirth. As you review your past, you may be tempted to judge where you've come from, the decisions you've made, and your past and current relationship to today's issue. The process of growth by its very nature entails both creation and destruction. Nature's gift to us is to expand to embrace the entire cycle of life. At this point, I would like you to take up your pen one final time and write a letter to the problem you brought with you to this day. I want you to acknowledge the role this issue has played in your life from the past up through the present moment. The pain it has caused you—and the payoffs and contributions it has made to your growth. Above all, I ask you to forgive your problem. Because of this problem, your mind may have wandered far afield, into judgment or fear or confusion, but the unseen order was present even in these states. It has always been with you. Where could you have gone to avoid it? It has been with you through this entire day and will see you through all the way to resolution.

You have been on this journey a long, long time. Sometimes you felt you could not go on—but you always did. And you've learned so much from your experiences. You've learned how strong you are. How resourceful. How able you are to learn from the things that happen to you and move forward again. You have learned about your capacity to love—and to set limits. How to risk—and how to protect yourself. You have learned to fail—and to rebound. When you must act—and when you must accept. And you have learned compassion. You could not have learned these things any other way. Nothing has been wasted. No lost opportunities. You are exactly where you need to be right now.

It is true that sometimes you must walk alone with your yearning for a while. But see how moments of resolution gently come and go, running side by side with you for a time, parting, and crossing again. Do you yearn for meaningful expression—a way to make a contribution through your work and life? Possibilities abound every step of the way. Sometimes it will be easy to see what you should be doing; sometimes the path leads back into the fog and the dark. But you've been through the rough patches before. You will emerge on the other side. And remember the excitement you feel when you do? Every time the fog clears, you realize that even while submerged, your capacity for life expanded.

So forgive your problem. Forgive it now. Bring everything you've got—everything you feel—all your aspirations, all your yearnings, to the process. When you have completed your letter. Return to this page.

✳

Albert Einstein once wrote that *"there are only two ways to live your life. One is as though nothing is a miracle. The other is as though everything is a miracle."*

At this point, I am going to ask you to complete your active role in this day's *Solved by Sunset* process. While there is more to come, this is the last task of the day in which your individual self will be invoked. This process will leave you whole—whether it be totally full or totally empty.

Soon you will have a choice to make. Whichever path you choose is the right one for you. There is no right and no wrong. There is only listening to your inner knowing, and doing what you must. Whichever choice you make, your personal ritual will complete your day's work: the creation of an environment in which conscious alignment with the unseen order is most likely to transpire.

Here is your first option. You may release the letter and your problem to the care of the unseen order. If you choose to release the letter, use the method that feels most natural to you. You may set it aflame in your fireplace, throw it into the ocean, tuck it into the bark of a favorite tree—or use any other means of release that occurs to you at this time. Stay with the process until your heart tells you you're done. Then go on to the next chapter of this book.

Your alternative is to embrace the letter and install it in a special way and place in your life, a reminder of where you've come from —and where you're headed. Roll it in a scroll or mount it in a prominent location where it will remind you of the experiences you've had here today. When you are through, turn to the next and final process of this book.

Eighteen

Holy

In the Book of Ezekiel, the Hebrew prophet makes reference to seraphim: mystical spirits whose function it is in the celestial hierarchy to praise God's holiness. "Holy Holy Holy" they repeat in constant adoration of the divine. Tradition explains that the Hebrew word *seraphim* is linked to the word for "flame." This is because the seraphim's experience of the divine is so intense that they can only get through the first "Holy" before they are burned up by the intensity of their devotion.

As you may recall, William James teaches us that there are two ways in which it is possible to deal with anger, worry, fear, despair, and so on in order to become more fully aligned with the unseen order of the universe. "One is that an opposite affection should overpoweringly break over us and the other is by getting so exhausted with the struggle that we have to stop." Today you have devoted much of your time engaging in the struggle. By now you have most probably exhausted your intellect as well as your emotions. Now, at this final stage of the seventh-hour process, you are going to shift gears. You are ready to invite the unseen order to overpoweringly break over you. In preparation, I would like to remind you how William James felt about the resolution of one's issues. He called relief from one's problems "a more commonplace happiness." He told of a state in which we are no longer looking for escape, but for more life.

How do you attain this state? As you know, this is not something you can make happen. You can only create the environment in which such an experience may transpire. You can only make yourself willing to receive. This is what the final hour's process is about.

You may recall our discussion in chapters 4 and 5 about the five stages one undergoes when traversing the void. Remember, that while I have numbered them, they are not linear. Each contains all the others and at any stage all may be simultaneously experienced. The stages are:

1. The Willingness to Descend

This you have shown yourself able to do by staying with this day's process through some very difficult and challenging inner terrain. You could not have done so if you had not been willing to consider the possibility that the fact that you have problems that result in pain, indecision, and vulnerability was not about what was wrong with you, but about what was right. Your cognitive structures were indeed yearning for a more mature organization. Today you have been using your right-brain capabilities, your emotions, and your spirituality to give you a point of contact with the unseen order, expressing itself as both entry into your own deeper material, and into richer communion with a loving, if mysterious, universe. By becoming willing to bring as much of yourself as you have to the

Solved by Sunset process today, you have proven yourself willing to engage in a struggle worthy of you.

2. Unconditional Surrender

You have taken the next step every time you resisted your urge to push away from your pain and became willing to jump into it. You have become willing to experience your broader range of internal possibilities more fully, trusting that by letting go of the old structures, you are making the space for something better to take its place.

3. Demand One's Rights

You have learned that you have the right to have a relationship with the unseen order of the universe that makes sense of your life. You have the right to ask for what you want of God—to ask the big questions and feel the big emotions. You have a faith so strong that you now realize that even your darker emotions will be embraced by the divine. You can express your anger at the injustice of the universe—your own humanity and the cruelties of creation. When you are suffering—and when you feel the pain of others—you bring to your complaints the knowledge that you have the right to feel as you do. You let your heart break open, and you provide a passageway for your fellow human beings—and for the unseen powers—to infuse you with love and support.

4. Transfiguration

You are open as never before to the possibility of transfiguration. Transfiguration occurs the moment you become willing to engage fully with your life at whatever level your life presents itself to you. You let go of your left-brain efforts to control and manipulate, to make things happen, trying, working, figuring things out, making an effort, preserving, and protecting—and become absolutely ordinary. At this stage, resolution comes spontaneously when you let go of your illusions—the desires and the expectations, particularly the expectation that tells you how spiritual you are, how far you've come, how important your contribution will be. You understand that you do not need to do extraordinary things in order to fit into the unseen order of the universe. You already do.

5. Emergence

Renewed and revitalized, you spontaneously emerge from the darkness, eager to participate in all of your life from a new, enhanced perspective. With supreme faith, you have a sense of the universe working through you toward some greater purpose, often in ways mysterious, beyond either your understanding or your control. You have the visceral experience of knowing fully that, given who you are, where you've come from, and the circumstances you face, you are in exactly the right place and time doing precisely what you need to be doing. You spontaneously engage with the unseen order of the universe, trusting that there are forces acting on your behalf every moment of your life.

✳

All of these stages converge in our seventh-hour's final exercise, the most powerful of all the processes I will be sharing with you today. It is a process that completes the switch from thinking with your analytical left brain to tapping the inner resources of your spiritual-intuitive right brain. It is the most completely efficient way I have encountered to switch your brain's channels from left to right.

It is called prayer.

But not the kind of prayer you are most probably accustomed to

—words of supplication or commitment. It's not even words of gratitude. The prayer I am going to be asking you to engage in has one purpose and one purpose, alone: to open your heart to the willingness to receive.

The prayer I will be teaching you contains elements inspired by the Centering Prayer, a method developed by Father Thomas Keating, a Cistercian priest, monk, and abbot, combined with ritual elements I have drawn from Native American, Zen, and the Judeo-Christian tradition.

It begins with your selection of a sacred word or phrase—any word or phrase that expresses to you your experience of a power greater than yourself. It may be "Loving Universe," "Peace," "God," or any other word or phrase that reminds you of your willingness to engage with divine presence.

Keating writes:

> The word is a sacred word because it is the symbol of your intention to open yourself to the mystery of God's presence beyond thoughts, images, or emotions. It is chosen not for its content but for its intent. It is merely a pointer that expresses the direction of your inner movement toward the presence of God.

After you have your sacred word in mind, find the best place for this ritual to transpire. If possible, find a spot that faces the horizon, where sunset will be taking place. If sunset has already occurred, or if you are in a situation where it will be impossible to participate directly with sunset—perhaps you are in a windowless room, or the weather is inhospitable—seat yourself before the dying embers in your fireplace, or the flame of a candle.

The next step of this prayer is to create a circle around you. If you are outdoors, you may draw a circle with a stick in the dirt or build the circle out of rocks. Indoors, you may circle yourself with favorite books or sacred objects. Alternately, you can simply imagine a circle of light surrounding you.

When you have completed your circle, sit down in the middle of it and relax the focus of your eyes and mind. Don't look at anything in particular or think about anything specific. What then? Simply this: you wait. If you begin to get anxious, or feel desire or anticipation welling up in you, repeat your sacred word in order to remind yourself to let go of your thoughts and feelings and return to silence. Whenever your mind or emotions wander, use your sacred word to gently guide you back.

The I Ching describes the state you are entering:

> Wait in the calm strength of patience. The time will fulfill itself. One need not fear lest strong will should not prevail; the main thing is not to expend one's powers prematurely in an attempt to obtain by force something for which the time is not yet ripe.

How long do you wait? And what, exactly, are you waiting for? The answer is this: You will know what you are waiting for when you become aware of already having received it and you will find yourself willing to wait for however long it takes.

Sunset
and
Beyond

Nineteen

Your Ordinary Self Is Enough

*As a classic Zen parable goes,
a novice monk approached his master, Joshu.
"I beg you to tell me something. What is the the key to
understanding everything? The secret to enlightenment?"
Joshu turned to him.
"Have you already eaten your meal this evening?"
"Yes, I've eaten," the young monk replied.
Joshu replied, "Now wash your bowl."*

In 1938, Barbara Ueland, author of *If You Want to Write: A Book About Art, Independence, and Spirit,* discovered that her greatest creativity, her breakthroughs, the resolution of her issues and problems, came as the result of the long, slow five or six miles she walked in the countryside near her home every day.

Euland writes: "It is only in walks that are a little too long that one has any new ideas."

Smart, energetic, do it now, pushing people so often say "I am
not creative." They are, but they should be idle, limp and alone
for much of the time, as lazy as men fishing on a levee, and
quietly looking and thinking, not willing all the time. This
quiet looking and thinking is the imagination; it is letting in
ideas. Willing is doing something you know already, something
you have been told by somebody else; there is no new imagina-
tive understanding in it. And presently, your soul gets fright-
fully sterile and dry because you are so quick, snappy and
efficient about doing one thing after another that you have no
time for your own ideas to come in and develop and gently
shine.

As Ueland walks, all alone, she absorbs the sky, lake, and trees around
her, neck and jaw loose, and as she walks, she repeats this mantra to
herself: "There is nothing to hurry about . . . I am free."

This is the kind of freedom Joshu was teaching his novice monk,
as have the many teachers we have encountered together during this
day, from William James to Einstein, from St. Augustine to the
Tibetan hermit Milarepa. Today you have had an experience of the
kind of freedom Ueland writes about. You have, for one day, managed to escape from the persistent chatter of your make-it-happen
left-brain consciousness to bask in the luxury of ideas not yet fully
formed, dreams yearning to express themselves, divine presence
beckoning to be received.

I began this book with a quote from Havelock Ellis: *"It is the
infinite for which we hunger, and we ride gladly on every little wave that
promises to bear us toward it."*

I trust that having experienced this for yourself today, you better
understand the underlying belief upon which this book is based: that
the resolution of your problems and issues will be the by-product of
your willingness to engage in the fully lived life. Whatever keeps
you from experiencing your alignment with the universe, the place

where resolution spontaneously occurs, is accidental and can be overcome. You have seen now for yourself that unhealthiness, rigidity, and ignorance are correctable problems. Breakthroughs, insight, and wisdom are not exceptional occurrences, but rather your natural state: the experience you can have the very moment you understand that your ordinary self is enough.

Already, you have proven yourself capable of establishing an environment in which the process of harmoniously adjusting yourself to the unseen order is most likely to transpire. But you have done so when you had a specific problem or issue on your mind. The gauntlet I lay at your feet is this: Are you willing to live this way every day of your life?

If you endeavor to soar above all obstacles, proclaiming as you have in the past to let nothing get in your way, you will become brittle and reactive. You may inadvertently set yourself against the universe, increasing rather than decreasing resistance by the very nature of your arrogant stance. A more productive attitude is to proclaim that you are going to do whatever it takes to succeed, understanding that many things are going to get in your way. *The I Ching* teaches you the way to do this. You must be ever vigilant to set your life in order and search your heart "lest it harbor any secret opposition to the will of God."

Rather than attack your problem as if it were an enemy to be conquered, take your inspiration from water. *The I Ching* explains that water sets the example for us:

> It flows on and on, and merely fills up all the places through which it flows; it does not shrink from any dangerous spot nor from any plunge, and nothing can make it lose its own essential nature. It remains true to itself under all circumstances.

Can you proclaim to God that you are willing to do whatever it takes to achieve resolution, understanding that "whatever" takes into consideration the care and well-being of your spirit? Can you have faith that your spirit will prevail, even as you accept that many things are going to get in your way? The key is not to place your focus on the achievement of perfection, but for you to grow large enough to encompass everything that transpires, including the imperfection. Creativity is an organic, life-driven process, and the process of new creation not only allows but demands periodic bouts of chaos and uncertainty. You mull over possibilities, take risks, sort out the vital from the trivial. Right-brain thinking when truly understood as an entry into rather than protection from the fully lived life is disorderly. You must keep at readiness your willingness to struggle with issues, to put your best thinking and solutions, your truest insights, and even your highest hopes to the test.

When you have depleted your inner resources, as you will from time to time, you will have one option yet remaining: the strength to be simple.

Katagiri Roshi, a Zen monk of contemporary times, once shared with his students just how great a challenge this can be.

"During the last *sesshin,* while we were sitting, I found myself thinking, 'Is this all I'm going to do with my life: just sit?' Then I caught it. Another thought."

Fate loves emptiness and simplicity and rushes into the void with light and love. When in doubt, do a little too much in the direction of the ordinary, and you will hit the mark.

It is likely that in your life you cannot take a full day out of your routines in order to do a process, such as the one you participated in today, every time you have a problem. You may not have the capability or willingness to set your routine commitments and involvements aside in order to live the life of a monk or mystic.

Is there some way, however, that you can reconnect to the deeper level of experience you participated with today when the need or opportunity arises? A way to short-circuit your left-brain processes to let the right-brain's intuitive knowing emerge?

You can. There's one final process I would like to share with you today. It consists of asking yourself a single question:

What is possible?

What is *possible*—how much can you give, how much can you accomplish, before you must stop to refuel? What compromises can you make—which will damage your spirit? What is *possible,* given that while you have responsibility, there are forces at play larger than yourself in your life and in the universe? What is *possible:* what can you change—what must you accept?

And at the same time, what is *possible*—when you give up beating down your spirit with busy little thoughts, freeing your vital energy to create rather than protect? What is *possible*—when you let go of old systems and structures that no longer work for you, and free your life to discover its new size and shape? What is *possible*—when you call upon your highest aspirations, willing to make sacrifices and to pay the price faith demands, in order to be fully alive? What is *possible* —when your heart is so full that the love and gratitude you feel overflow your boundaries to spontaneously, effortlessly brighten the lives of others? What is possible—when your spirit grows larger than your fear, and you find it within yourself to step out of the status quo and into the unknown?

I envision a society of men and women who are consciously aware of the creative dissonances inherent in the consideration of what we have accomplished versus what is possible—human beings who are on an inner journey to a place where moral values take precedence over the pursuit of comfort. I envision a society of people who leave time for their relationships—to relax and to have fun, to care sincerely for one another. I envision a society of individuals willing to struggle with the imperfection of humanity, and yet who work, dream, and believe in the potential of the human community to be better than it has thus far shown itself to be. And I envision a time when people of all faiths participate together in a wholistically transcendent experience of the divine, a unity great enough to encompass us all.

It is here, in mystical experience, that we participate as equals with the unseen order of the universe. This is the ultimate freedom —and it is available to you and to every one of us. Once you have experienced this—you will be fundamentally transformed.

You may recall that at the start of this day, I quoted William James on the issue of the human potential: "There are higher and lower limits of possibility set to each personal life." Only when we are willing to "touch our own upper limit and live in our own highest center of energy" can we hope to fulfill the spiritual potential of our lives. You have to be willing to play the game of life from a place where the fulfillment of your spiritual potential is possible or life seems flat and hopeless.

I hope and trust that the original problem you brought into this day has been resolved during the course of the many processes you have undergone. You should be pleased with all that you have accomplished. But I hope that along the way, you have gained something even more valuable: a glimpse into the mysterious and divine laws of the universe.

In the Bible's story of creation, the setting sun did not signify the end of the day just passing, but rather the beginning of the new day. As the sun goes down on the problem you brought with you for resolution, let it take with it that which you no longer need or want in your life. What is the biggest belief you carried into this day that you now realize you have outgrown? Whose opinion about how you are doing in your life do you no longer want or need? What beliefs did you grow up with that you do not need to carry into the future? What would it mean to you to let these things go? It's all right if you feel bittersweet sadness right now: the beliefs that the sun is taking away with it have been with you a long, long time. But as the last rays of sun recede into the night, ask yourself: *How might things be different for me now?*

Just as you are not the same person who sat down at the beginning of this day to do the *Solved by Sunset* process, neither will you return to your life and the world as you last left it. The universe is in a state of constant change. You can never know what is going to happen to you—not even one moment from now. Remember the rainmaker I told you about earlier today? While he was doing the contemplative work of removing his inner resistances to alignment with the unseen order, even before he got to the point of carrying out the rainmaking ceremony, it started to pour. Such was the power of his commitment that the resolution of his internal process swept along the rectification of the climate in its wake.

Soon you will be reentering your everyday life—but with new perceptions, knowledge, and capabilities. Know that regardless of the results you feel you have or have not achieved today, you have done exactly what was called for in your life right now. By cultivating your inner world, you are planting seeds that are already growing in their vitality and energy. At any moment, you can become aware of having renewed purpose, unexpected insight, and breakthroughs.

Let the setting sun take with it your resistance, your doubts, your willful efforts to keep control. But let it leave with you that which you realize you are no longer willing to surrender: your right to a relationship with the universe that makes sense of your existence; the heroism inherent in the fully lived life; and, above all, the possibility of miracles.

Prepare to be surprised.

The
Solved by Sunset
Process:
A Summary

The Four Assumptions

One:
There is an unseen order in the universe.

Two:
*Your highest good lies in harmoniously adjusting yourself
to this unseen order.*

Three:
*Whatever keeps you from experiencing your alignment with the
universe is accidental, and can be overcome.*

Four:
*Forces beyond your comprehension are already engaged in
your problem-solving process.*

Hour Number One:
Setting Your Intention

What is your intention for today? What is the problem or issue that is on your mind and what is it you would truly hope to accomplish? For the next ten minutes, write nonstop, never taking your pen off your paper. Write as fast as you can. Write anything that comes into your mind. Don't lead your thoughts, follow them.

Hour Number Two:
Bracketing the Descent

Experience your emotions fully for an hour. Play some evocative music on your stereo. If you've got a fireplace, throw on a log. Shut the doors so that you will have total privacy. Go as deeply into your feelings as you are able. Don't write. Don't read. Don't do anything but feel. If you are concerned about falling apart, set an alarm clock to let you know when your hour's descent will end.

Hour Number Three:
Putting Your Problem in Context

Answer this series of questions in order to find the threads of meaning underlying your original mythology—and to see if you can find the roots of your current problem in the solutions of your own past.

1. **What is your earliest happy memory?**

2. **What interrupted that happiness?**

3. **What was your solution?**

4. **What good came of your solution?**

5. **What price did you have to pay for this solution?**

6. How is it that the thing you sacrificed so long ago is still effecting you? How does it relate to the problem you want to resolve today?

After you have answered these six questions, write the myth of your life. Begin each of five key paragraphs with these words:

1. Once upon a time, there was a happy child named . . .

2. Then something terrible happened . . .

3. The brave little child knew what had to be done . . .

4. And they all lived happily ever after . . .

5. The moral of this story is . . .

Ask yourself: Does the moral of the myth you just wrote down resolve your current problem? If not, try writing a new ending to your story. You can use the same beginning and development you used in the myth above, parts 1 and 2. But try out new possibilities for parts 3 to 5 until your hero gets the result he or she truly deserves: one that will work for you now.

Hour Number Four: Thunderstruck

During this hour, ask four specific questions about the problem you would like to resolve by sunset. The questions are these:

1. What is the truth about the problem or issue I am facing in my life right now?

2. What is the nature of the obstacle that is in the way of resolving this problem by sunset tonight?

3. What should I do?

4. What outcome can I expect?

Choose from among four tools to assist you in this process. You can use one or any combination. The tools are:

1. Divination, used as an intuitive decision-making tool. There are two stipulations. The first is that you put aside any instruction booklets explaining the meaning of the symbology. Instead, you are only to ask yourself what each card or symbol means to you. The second stipulation is that if you ever pull a card or cast a reading that feels wrong to you, throw it back to try again—or put this option aside and out of your thoughts.

2. Go to a favorite book, perhaps the Bible or some other favorite spiritual work, and with question in mind, open at random and begin to read.

3. Take your question for a walk in nature. As you stroll, remain receptive to personally meaningful signs in the environment.

4. Take your question into a closed-eye meditation or perhaps even into a deep sleep where you will be asking for a dream. (Don't forget to set your alarm clock to wake you at the end of the hour.) If you have a dream, write down any of the images immediately upon awakening. If you choose the guided visualization, close your eyes and imagine a wise being coming to you with a present. When you receive the gift, envision opening it and seeing what is inside. Allow yourself to be surprised by it.

Hour Number Five: Dialogue with Your Inner Voices

Bring the problem you would like to resolve by sunset tonight before your inner board of directors and ask them to reach a consensus of what will work best for you. If you already have a solution to your problem, ask that board member to speak up first. If not, Critic will be the kick-off speaker. Write down both your questions and comments:

Will the first voice please tell us: What position have you taken in relation to the problem I want to solve by sunset? Do you have some satisfying resolution in mind? If so, what is it? If not—what is getting in the way?

What does Critic have to say about this?

What does the nurturing voice have to say about this?

What does the inner child have to say about this?

Is there anybody else who would like to offer his or her opinion at this time, about any of the previous speakers—or about my role as chairman of the board?

It's time for us to hear from our special counsel, Higher Self. Higher Self, having heard all these voices, what is your opinion now? If you previously sent me a sign, symbol, or dream image I did not fully understand, now is the time to reveal to me the significance of it. What does it mean? What guidance are you trying to give to me?

If consensus has been reached, thank your board members and call this session to its conclusion. If not, open the floor for discussion. When you are finished, conclude with the following statement: Board Members, Higher Self, I would like to thank you for your time and trouble on this matter. Meeting adjourned.

Hour Number Six: Eleven Questions

1. What issue would you most like to resolve right now?

2. What outcome would you most like to achieve?

3. How have you tried to resolve this situation so far?

4. What was it about this approach that did not work?

5. What payoff or benefit have you received from having this situation in your life?

6. What other way could you get the same payoff that would be better for you?

7. What can you change about this situation?

8. What must you accept about this situation?

9. What is your greatest fear about this situation?

10. What is the truth about this situation?

11. What one thing are you now willing to do to get the resolution you seek?

Hour Number Seven Until Sunset: Ready to Receive

1. Read through your day's writing to remember your experiences, to check in on how you felt about your problem, yourself, and this process before—and how you feel about it at the present time.

2. Write a letter to your problem acknowledging the role it has played in your life. Forgive your problem, seeing in it the mysterious workings of the unseen order of the universe.

3. Release the letter by setting it aflame in your fireplace or any other means of release that occurs to you. Or embrace the letter, installing it in a special place or way in your life—a reminder of where you've come from and where you're headed.

4. Open your heart to the willingness to receive through a centering prayer. Begin by selecting a sacred word—any word that expresses to you your experience of a power greater than yourself. After you have your sacred word in mind, find a spot for this prayer ritual to transpire. If possible, find a place that faces the sunset. The next step

is to create a circle around you. If you are outdoors, you may draw a circle with a stick in the dirt or build the circle out of rocks. Indoors, you may use favorite books or sacred objects. Alternately, you can simply imagine a circle of light surrounding you. When you have completed your circle, sit down in the middle of it and relax the focus of your eyes and mind. Don't look at anything in particular or think about anything specific. What then? Simply this: you wait. If you begin to get anxious, or feel desire or anticipation welling up in you, repeat the sacred word in order to remind yourself to let go of your thoughts and feelings and return to silence. How long do you wait, and what, exactly, are you waiting for? You will know what you are waiting for when you become aware of having already received it—and you will find yourself willing to wait for however long it takes.

What Is
Possible?

Sources

Anthony, Carol K. *The Philosophy of the I Ching*. Stow, Mass.: Anthony Publishing, 1981.

Batson, Daniel C.; Patricia Schoenrade; and Larry W. Ventis. *Religion and the Individual: A Social-Psychological Perspective*. New York: Oxford University Press, 1993.

Borysenko, Joan, Ph.D. *Fire in the Soul*. New York: Warner, 1993.

Bregman, Lucy. *The Rediscovery of Inner Experience*. Chicago: Nelson-Hall Publishing, 1982.

Byrnes, Joseph F. *The Psychology of Religion*. New York: Free Press, 1984.

Campbell, Joseph (in conversation with Michael Toms). *An Open Life*. Burdett, N.Y.: Larson Publications, 1988.

Carroll, Robert P. *When Prophecy Failed: Cognitive Dissonance in the Prophetic Traditions of the Old Testament*. New York: Seabury Press, 1979.

Chodron, Pema. *Start Where You Are: A Guide to Compassionate Living*. Boston: Shambhala Publishing, 1994.

Eliade, Mircea, ed. *The Encyclopedia of Religion*. New York: Macmillan, 1987.

Feinstein, David, Ph.D., and Stanley Krippner, Ph.D. *Personal Mythology*. New York: Tarcher, 1988.

James, William. *The Varieties of Religious Experience: A Study in Human Nature. Introduction by Reinhold Niebuhr*. New York: Collier Books, 1961.

Jung, Carl G. *Man and His Symbols*. Garden City, N.Y.: Doubleday, 1964.

Keen, Sam and Anne Valley Fox. *Telling Your Story*. Garden City, New York: Doubleday, 1973.

Lindbergh, Anne Morrow. *Gift From the Sea*. New York: Vintage Books, 1978.

Marrs, Donald. *Executive in Passage*. Los Angeles: Barrington Sky Publishing. 1990.

May, Rollo. *The Cry for Myth*. New York: W. W. Norton, 1991.

Phillips, Dorothy Berkley. *The Choice is Always Ours*. New York: R. B. Smith, 1948.

Sawyer, F. A. *Prophecy and the Prophets of the Old Testament*. New York: Oxford University Press, 1987.

Stone, Hal, Ph.D., and Sidra Winkleman, Ph.D. *Embracing Ourselves*. San Rafael, Calif.: New World Library, 1989.

Telushkin, Rabbi Joseph. *Jewish Wisdom*. New York: William Morrow, 1994.

Toppel, Edward Allen. *Zen in the Markets: Confessions of a Samurai Trader*. New York: Warner Books, 1994.

Ueland, Barbara. *If You Want to Write: A Book About Art, Independence and Spirit*. Saint Paul, Minn.: Graywolf Press, 1987.

Ward, James. *Thus Says the Lord*. Nashville: Abington Press, 1991.

Weiner, Herbert. *9 and 1/2 Mystics: The Kabbala Today*. Foreword by Elie Wiesel. New York: Collier Books, 1969 (1992 edition published by Macmillan Publishing Co.)

Wilhelm, Richard, and Cary F. Baynes. *The I Ching*. Foreword by Carl Jung. Princeton, N.J.: Princeton University Press, 1950.

Doing What's Next

If you would like a free membership to Overachiever's Anonymous, and to be on Carol Orsborn's mailing list, send a SASE to Overachiever's Anonymous, P.O. Box 159061, Nashville, Tennessee 37215. OA was founded on a platform promising no meetings, classes, or fundraisers in perpetuity.

Author's Note

Members of Overachiever's Anonymous have contributed case histories and anecdotal support for the principles shared in this book. When requested, I have honored their desire for anonymity by changing personal and company names and fictionalizing details.